If You Can't **Manage** Them You Can't **Teach** Them

Advice for Running a Chaos-Free Classroom Where Middle and High School Students Can Really Learn

Kim Campbell with Dr. Kay Herting Wahl

*Incentive*Publications

BY WORLD BOOK

This book is dedicated to all my children—who are loaned to me each year, and whom I love unconditionally. Without a doubt, my students have been my greatest teachers, and for that I will be forever grateful.

Illustrated by Kathleen Bullock
Cover by Debbie Weekly

Print Edition ISBN 978-0-86530-513-7
E-book Edition ISBN 978-1-62950-030-0 (PDF)

World Book, Inc.
180 North LaSalle Street
Suite 900
Chicago, Illinois 60601
U.S.A.

For information about World Book and Incentive Publications products, call **1-800-967-5325,** or visit our websites at **www.worldbook.com** and **www.incentivepublications.com.**

Revised printing.
Printed in the United States of America by LSC Communications, Willard, OH
2nd printing April 2017

Contents

Who's the manager?

✔ A Personal Reflection on Conflict

In order to better understand yourself as a classroom manager, take some time to explore these questions. Jot some notes in response.

1. How did your parents discipline you? (Were they direct? passive? aggressive? passive-aggressive? Who was the authority figure?)

2. When you manage your own children or students, what techniques do you use that you learned from your parents? Or what do you do differently from your parents?

3. What is your style for handling conflict in your personal life?

   Avoiding (You avoid the situation for several days before addressing the conflict.)

   Assertive (You address the situation soon after the event has happened. You are calm and able to discuss what happened.)

   Peace-making (You do everything possible to avoid conflict, even if it means you do not address the situation.)

   Aggressive (You confront the situation right as it is happening. If people get angry, that's okay, as long as you have a chance to say your piece.)

   Passive-Aggressive (You do not directly confront the situation but avoid the person, making sarcastic comments, or show subtle signs of hostility or aggression.)

4. Do you handle conflict in the same manner with both males and females? If not, how does your handling of conflict with males and females differ?

5. Do you handle conflict differently with persons of different ethnic backgrounds? If not, how does your handling of conflict differ from person to person?

6. When you are in a conflict, what do you fear most?

In the beginning , they scared me—these young adolescents I had agreed to teach. They said and did weird things, such as . . .

> *. . . the time Bryan came up to me and asked, "Ms. Campbell, what is your last name?" (I thought to myself, "Is this really happening?" That was just before I thought to myself, "What was I thinking when I decided to be a middle school teacher?")*

> *. . . or the time that Clareese began dancing, alone, in the center of the room— swaying back and forth with not a care in the world. (This was while I was presenting a scintillating geography lesson with great flair.) When I asked, "Clareese, what on earth are you doing?" she answered, "Oh, sorry, Ms. C, I'm just not used to free time, so I thought I would try this." (Free time?)*

> *. . . or the time a student told me to "!*$#% off" and threw a chair, right at the high point of my dynamic interactive lecture on colonialism. (How COULD he?) Maybe he had snooped into my lesson plans and noticed that I had labeled my teaching strategy as interactive—and thought cursing and chair-throwing was part of the plan.*

> *. . . and the time when a student (I'll not divulge the name), exiting my 5th- period class, swore that he would come after me when school ended that day.*

I struggled to figure out how to manage these "squirrels on amphetamines" (as they had been described to me). I thought I was the only teacher who was dazed and confused. But I now know that I had company. Most middle level and high school teachers take a college course or two on discipline or classroom management. But for most of us, the realities of handling the students and getting along with them (not to mention helping them get along with each other) while actually trying to teach them something, only sink in when we are actually on the job. By about the fourth day, we discover that 90% of the job is managing kids—finding ways to keep

If You Can't Manage Them . . .

everyone moving in some sane pattern with little interruption. And when we new teachers figure this out, we spend the next three months wondering why in the world we took this job!

• • • • • • • •

Whether you have been teaching a few days or several years (and whether you teach elementary, middle school, or high school), you have undoubtedly figured this out: You may be highly intelligent. You may have had a perfect GPA in teacher training or grad school. You may be able to design creative, compelling, well-organized lessons. **But if you can't manage the students, you can't teach them.** There is plenty of research documenting the various connections between classroom climate and student performance. But no middle school teacher or high school teacher that I know needs research to convince her or him of this truth: If you fail to run a classroom that operates fairly smoothly with a minimum of disruptions and bad behavior, there will be little effective learning.

Beyond the drawbacks for students, consistent frustration with student behavior leads to teacher burnout. Student misbehavior is reported as one of the primary reasons teachers leave the profession (Grayson and Alvarez, 2007; Ingersoll, 2001). Improved learning experiences for students, more joy for teachers, and a decrease in discipline problems and classroom interruptions—these are more than ample reasons to work toward satisfying and satisfactory classroom management.

Discipline issues at the middle school and high school levels have increased in recent years. There has been a dramatic rise in rates of misbehavior, suspension, and expulsion at the middle school level (Skiba, 2000). Middle level and secondary teachers are less able to manage difficult student behavior than Elementary school teachers (Baker, 2005). Seventh-grade students with a history of discipline problems are at high likelihood for becoming at-risk or dropping out of school by ninth grade (Murdock, Anderman, and Hodge, 2000).

The #1 Factor in Classroom Management

You may think that kids' misbehavior is the major component of classroom management. This certainly accounts for the most frustration, time, and energy. You may blame the parents who aren't involved in their kids' education enough, aren't setting limits, or aren't helping kids be responsible. You may think it's the current culture with its media messages, attitudes toward learning, lure of getting something without working for it, poverty, hopelessness, apathy, distractions of technology, or any number of other cultural conditions that contribute to misbehavior in the classroom. Many teachers see their schools as having inconsistent (or no) policies regarding student behavior, and blame the system for the increasing struggles with discipline and student attitudes. YES! All this stuff contributes to problems in the classroom. But if you are going to have a safe, comfortable, orderly (mostly) classroom climate in which students can learn well—you will need to come face to face with the key ingredient in effective (or ineffective) classroom management. And that is not the students. It is none of the other things listed. It is YOU, the teacher.

If You Can't Manage Them . . .

I believe that YOUR classroom management is rooted in who you are as a person. YOU bring all these to school with you: your personal out-of-school experiences, your relationships, your history, and your tendencies. This is why I began this chapter with the reflection on page 6. Take a few minutes to go back and review your notes on that page. How you handle conflict in your life plays a **HUGE** role in the classroom manager you become.

> The students move on, but you stay. And the patterns that aren't working? They stay, too.

Students come and, as the school year ends, they go. Your most troublesome students will be in someone else's class. But the management issues you had last year with student X or Y or Z still will be with you when those kids are gone. That's because the students move on, but you stay. And the patterns that aren't working? They stay, too.

If you work with preadolescents or adolescents, conflict WILL be part of your classroom life! There will be conflict with them and between them. In order to establish an effective management style, you must examine your relationship to conflict. You will have a tendency to handle conflict and issues in the classroom (and with your colleagues and parents at school) in the same way you manage these in your life outside school. This is particularly true in highly tense or uncomfortable situations. Do you avoid confrontation? Try to get away from conflict— at all costs? Keep your cool? Ignore or downplay anger, aggression, or conflict? Lose your temper? Give up? Give in? Respond immediately and directly, with little emotion? Get away, think about things, and confront later? Feel paralyzed? Feel personally attacked? Do you threaten? Get defensive? Shout? Try to smooth it over? Whatever is your usual habit will probably be your fallback position as you manage students in the classroom.

You won't have the same reactions to all students.
Because you have different histories and relationships with different kinds of people, your management style will vary for different kinds of students. How do you handle conflict with males versus females? How do you handle conflict with people of a different race or culture? In my household, we never listened to our mother. But when our father spoke, we paid attention. So my tendency is to respond differently in conflict with males—male students, male colleagues, male authority figures. It will be natural for your reactions to vary for different genders, cultures, styles, attitudes, or personalities of students. But still, in each different situation, you will likely revert to the response that is most familiar.

MOTHER?

Who you were as a student affects your responses to your present students. There is a tendency to think that the best or right way for a student to be is the way we were as a student. For example, a teacher friend of mine can remember being in trouble only once in school—for something minor like handing in a paper in the wrong basket. Because he expects kids to be like he was as a student, he has a bunch of issues dealing with his students. He never anticipates student reactions, tricks, manipulations, work-avoidance tendencies, mischievousness, or misbehavior. So he is repeatedly blindsided by student behaviors. Now as for

If You Can't Manage Them . . .

me—I was the class clown, the entertainer. I was the kid who caused the trouble, who had all kinds of clever shenanigans up my sleeve and quick, funny comebacks. So I anticipate this kind of stuff. I often see trouble before it comes—and I'm ready for it. This may give me a slight advantage . . . but then, I have other habits and past experiences that I have to combat when I respond to student behavior.

Who you are affects every aspect of your management.
This YOU factor spreads way beyond situations of conflict.
Your whole management style and your relationships
with students are affected by . . .
- how YOU were disciplined
- how YOU feel about and respond to conflict
- experiences YOU had as a student
- how YOU felt about yourself as a student
- how YOU feel about students as a group
- how YOU feel about individuals in your class
- what YOU really believe about students
- how YOU feel about your competence as a teacher
- how YOU feel about your ability to manage students

This Is Good News!

Many years ago, a wise child psychologist, Haim Ginott, wrote a simple book with a powerful message for teachers (*Teacher & Child*, 1972). His message rescued many frazzled teachers from chaotic classrooms. This is a basic premise of his beliefs:

> *I've come to the frightening conclusion that I am the decisive element in the classroom. It's my personal approach that*

creates the climate. It's my daily mood that makes the weather. As a teacher, I possess tremendous power to make a student's life miserable or joyous. I can be a tool of torture or an instrument of inspiration. I can humiliate or humor, hurt or heal. In all situations it is my response that decides whether a crisis will be escalated or de-escalated and a student humanized or dehumanized (pg 13).

I can hear you thinking, "This is GOOD NEWS?" Yes, it is! We teachers can really make a difference in the lives of our students! We can combat all those influences that contribute to problems in the classroom! (See these back on page 9.) We can humor! We can heal! We can humanize! We can inspire! But we can only do so if we **get it**! Get what? Get that **we are the decisive element** in our classrooms! Fully believing that you, the teacher, are the root of successful classroom management, I want to share some ideas about what this means and what to do about it.

● ● ● ● Skip the Judgment

Don't be discouraged about any of your answers to the questions on the reflection at the beginning of this chapter. Don't be intimidated by the statement of Haim Ginott's "frightening conclusion" in the quote above. Don't feel guilty about any of your answers to the questions about how you handle conflict in your personal life (pages 10 and 11). I have not raised these questions to assign right or wrong, good or bad. So to get started on your journey of becoming a better classroom manager, leave self-judgment and self-criticism at the classroom door.

> Leave self-judgment and self-criticism at the classroom door.

● ● ● ● Be Aware

In the chapters that follow, there will be plenty of ideas and strategies for things such as running a smooth classroom, building good relationships with students, setting rules and procedures, enforcing consequences, and helping students develop inner discipline. But here, I begin the book by focusing on you, because I believe that you bring your whole self into the classroom—every day. The best thing you can do about that is to **be aware of what it is that you bring**. Ask yourself the kinds of questions I've asked in this chapter. Pay attention to the answers. This will help you select techniques to use with students. For example, if your tendency is to avoid conflict, you can plan ahead for situations in which you must directly address the conflict. And you can start practicing some techniques for meeting conflict head-on. If you tend to back off disciplining a girl when she turns into a drama queen, you can be ready with an approach that does not let unacceptable behavior go unaddressed. If you can think ahead and identify your fallback position in certain situations, you will not be caught off guard. You'll be ready.

● ● ● ● Check Your Attitude

Preadolescents and adolescents will pick up every attitude you have about them, about learning, about classroom life, and about your job as a teacher. They'll figure it out from the way you talk to them, the way you teach them, the way you discipline them, the amount of interest you show in them, what you expect from them, your body language, and from a hundred other signals and messages you send—many of them unintentional. As you examine what it is you bring to the classroom that will affect your management, do a thorough review of what it is you really believe about your students.

- Do you see students as significant?

- Do you see them as capable?

- Do you believe that they are able to be in control of their own lives?

- Do you truly accept every student?

- Do you believe that every one of them can learn and succeed?

- Do you want to know them?

- Are you appreciative of each one's uniqueness?

- Do you know and accept their developmental characteristics?

> A teacher who cares about me believes that I can do well—and helps me reach my goals.
> – Andre, grade 8

- Are you judgmental of their habits, attire, interests, fads, or passions?

- Do you like your job?

- Do you enjoy being with your students?

- Do you favor certain kinds of students?

- Are you afraid of any of them?

Take a hard look at your answers, and try to see yourself as your students will see you. Believe me, they will tune in to your attitudes. And if your attitudes are disapproving, annoyed, impatient, or discriminatory,

If You Can't Manage Them . . .

they will tune you out. You'll lose their confidence and connection, and this will spell trouble. Get an attitude adjustment where necessary. Keep your mind free of judgment and open to full appreciation of every student. This attitude will have a positive effect on your classroom management, I guarantee!

Be Real

Just as they have radar out for adult attitudes about them, students have a keen sense for authenticity. Some teachers put on a facade of what they think a teacher should be. No teacher can pretend care, interest, or respect without being detected. Talk in your normal voice, not a "pretend" teacher voice. Don't insult your students with an artificial self; they deserve to be educated by a genuine human being.

Take the Risk

I can't even count the number of teachers who have told me that being direct or firm is not their personality. They say that confronting behavior is just not "who they are." I believe them. I understand this! Certain behaviors do or do not come easily to certain personalities. But don't we ask our students to take academic risks every single day? Don't we ask them to expand their thinking? Don't we sometimes ask them to work with other students who may terrify them? We ask students to do many things not fitted to their "personality" or that are not "them" as a person. We ask them to overcome their fears and to experiment with new ways of acting or learning. Why should we as educators be any different? Why should we not have to change methods that don't work well or contribute to a good learning environment? Why should we not examine and adjust our personal styles in order to improve the learning and safety of our classrooms?

My former principal, Terry Wolfson, used to ask her struggling teachers the following question: "What are you getting out of the current situation that you are not willing to change?" (In other words, "What is stopping you from changing your current methods of classroom control?") I think this is a good question for all of us to ask. Then, I'll add these questions: "So, what are YOU willing to change in your management style to have a more effective classroom? What risks are YOU willing to take to ensure that all students have the same opportunity to learn?"

What are you willing to change in your management style to have a more effective classroom?

We all have different fears, motivations, and personalities; therefore, some of the suggestions in this book may not fit into your toolbox. Some may not match who you are. They may not seem to fit with your hesitations around classroom management. However, the "not matching" does not mean you should get off the hook with the excuse, "It's not who I am." Instead, be open-minded. Think about how, with some strategic changes, you can make each technique fit for you. I will provide a variety of practical strategies and techniques that you can add to your repertoire in the arena of classroom management. I have also offered some type of self-reflection opportunity to set the stage for each chapter. My hope is that by taking time to personally reflect on some issues

If You Can't Manage Them . . .

surrounding management, you will better understand your own style and philosophy for developing a safe and effective classroom. I encourage you to take the risks to do this kind of reflection. I encourage you to take risks to try new strategies—even if they are uncomfortable for you in the beginning.

How YOU Can Create Management Problems

Wait a minute! Isn't this a book to help reduce management problems? It is! A HUGE part of that goal is connected to understanding what teachers do to actually **create and increase** disturbances, issues, and problems in the classroom. So start your search for help with better classroom management by noticing what you might be doing that creates problems or makes a problem worse. I guarantee an increase in chaos and behavior problems if you follow these steps:

1. Fail to pay attention to what is happening in all corners of your room.
2. Don't take time to build relationships and community within your classroom.
3. Underestimate the importance of communicating well with parents.
4. Be disorganized or skimp on planning.
5. Be poorly prepared when the bell rings.
6. Let students sit wherever they want.
7. Respond inconsistently or intermittently to misbehavior.

8. Allow a situation or issue to get out of hand before you intervene.

9. Give little thought to the effects of the physical classroom arrangement.

10. Start the year with no established rules or routines for behavior or academics.

11. Fail to follow established rules or procedures consistently.

12. Do not establish clear consequences.

13. Leave students out of the discussion about what the rules and consequences of breaking them should be.

14. Don't anticipate challenges that might arise with a lesson.

15. Yell at students.

16. Call students out (discipline or scold) in front of their classmates.

OH, NO!
ONLY FIVE MINUTES
UNTIL CLASS STARTS!

17. Do not be direct with students. (Do not tell them specifically what you need them to do.)

18. Think that if you are nice, students will like you and therefore will behave.

19. Allow yourself to be drawn into power struggles with students.

20. Sit at your desk when the group is engaged in a discussion or lesson.

21. Sit at your desk when small groups are working.

22. Fail to recognize who the leaders are in each class.

23. Commit to use the exact same management strategies with all students.

24. Call a student's parents about an issue without first trying to work out the problem with the student.

25. Expect students to work long stretches of time without breaks, movement, or change of pace.

How YOU Can Prevent Management Problems

In his studies of effective and ineffective classroom managers, Jacob Kounin discovered that the key to successful management was not what teachers did to handle misbehavior. It was, instead, the strategies teachers used to prevent problems from occurring in the first place (Kounin, 1977). Here are some strategies that I know reduce management issues and avoid chaos:

1. Have eyes in the back of your head! (Be aware of everything going on!)

2. Be deliberate in building relationships with your students.

3. Be deliberate in planning community-building experiences for your class or team.

4. Find ways to communicate (frequently) with parents.

5. Be ultra organized.

6. Be fully prepared and ready to roll when the bell rings.

7. Seat students in arrangements that will reduce disruptions or problems.

8. Arrange classroom materials, furniture, and traffic patterns to reduce potential distractions and issues.

9. Set clear expectations for behavior and academics.

10. Establish and teach the routines and rules of your classroom.

11. Make sure consequences of misbehavior are clear and reasonable.

12. Respond consistently to misbehavior—according to established procedures.

13. Address a problematic situation **before** it gets out of hand.

14. Recognize that students **need** and **must have** breaks.

15. Plan ahead for transitions—how to make them in an orderly way, and how to end them.

16. Create lessons that are engaging and relevant.

17. Be consistent, firm, and fair when dealing with discipline issues.

18. Be direct and honest when redirecting students.

19. Do not be afraid to use appropriate humor.

20. Do not yell, blame, shame, threaten, belittle, bribe, preach, or discipline a student in front of classmates.

Be Yourself

The psychologist and educator Carl Rogers wrote:

> It is quite customary for teachers rather consciously to put on the mask, the role, the facade, of being a teacher, and to wear this facade all day, removing it only when they have left school at night (1969, pg 107).

Although his statement is fifty years old, it fits many teachers still today. Think about whether this applies at all to you. Leave your mask at home. Better yet, shred it!

A large portion of this chapter is titled "This Is Good News!"—remember? Here is some good more news: Jacob Kounin, classroom management researcher and theorist, studied the behaviors of effective and ineffective classroom managers. He concluded that success with classroom management is unrelated to the personality of the teacher. Instead, it is dependent upon technique (1977). Do you hear that? **It is NOT about your personality!** It is about what you do!

This means that whoever you are as a person, you can have the kind of classroom climate that you'd like! You don't have to be a comedian to use humor in your classroom. You don't have to be an aggressive person to handle issues directly and promptly. You don't have to be a natural therapist to build good relationships with students. You don't have to be anyone else, or try to adopt another personality. You just have to learn some techniques. This you can do! I'd like to offer some advice and techniques to help you—things I have learned from experience, from colleagues, and especially from my students.

SHOULD I WEAR THE HAPPY TEACHER MASK, OR THE SERIOUS-BUT-SINCERE MASK TODAY?

Don't start class without them!

I've Got Relationships, Right?

Check up on the status of relationships with your students.

1. You will need a list of your students. If the school year is just beginning, use a class list from last year. Choose a class period at random.

2. Write down something you know about each particular student. This cannot relate to what kind of student he or she is in your classroom. It could be about some interest, outside activity, family situation, hobbies, goals, or something else you know about the student.

3. How easy was this?

4. What kinds of things do you know about your students?

5. Look back over the list and write an X by the names of students for whom you hesitated or had a hard time identifying something. Is there anything you notice?

6. What did you learn from doing this?

You might be surprised at how much you really do know about your students, and you might also find yourself recognizing what you don't know. Any outcome of this activity is okay. Just keep this exercise in mind as you read through and respond to Chapter 2.

The environment in which my kids learn best and in which my kids ENJOY learning contains a teacher who "gets them"—that is, a teacher who conveys respect for their feelings and thoughts through his or her behavior and communication with the kids. Also, this teacher is someone who makes a personal connection with my kids by building a relationship with them. This doesn't just mean with my kid, either. It means that the teacher does this with all kids. My kid is watching all those interactions!

— Justina, parent of adolescents

On that first warm August school day, Chris entered my room with a vengeance. He strutted by me as I stood at the door. He did not say a word, but his message was loud and clear: He did not want to be here. He could care less about what I had to say. No one, including me, would tell him what to do.

The struggle was set that first day, and it persisted. I prayed for him to be absent. (Couldn't the child get a cold for just one day?) After weeks of frustration, I asked my assistant principal to mediate a conversation between the two of us. Yes, it took up my entire prep period, but it was one of the best decisions I had ever made regarding a child and his or her behavior.

Chris talked first. He said he felt that I did not like him. He said that he sensed my animosity every day from the moment he walked into my classroom. I knew Chris wasn't far from the truth, so I asked him what I had done to give him these messages. He said it was the way I looked at him, the fact that I sat him in the back of the room, and that several times I did not call on him when he had his hand in the air.

The mediation gave me a chance to explain that I did like him, but that he, too, was sending mixed messages to me about being in my class. After our conversation, I walked Chris back to his class. I asked him some questions about himself. In that short time, I learned about his love for his younger brother and for basketball. From then on, I mentioned something about basketball or checked in about his brother each time he entered class. I basically had begun to develop a safe relationship with Chris by talking with him about something other than school—by showing him that I had some interest in him as a person.

> No significant learning occurs without a significant relationship.
> –James Comer

My Deepest Bias

Caring, trusting relationships with students are absolutely the most important ingredient in an enjoyable, effective classroom. I cannot say this loudly or often enough. This is the foundation for joy and cooperation in your group! On a purely practical level, teachers will have far fewer discipline problems and struggles with students if they have nurtured good relationships with them. But the sheer avoidance of problems is just a small part of the reward. Far deeper, broader, more meaningful to students, more satisfying and more long lasting are all the human benefits. This includes (among many benefits) students liking themselves and their school experiences better, learning more, and achieving at higher levels academically.

Most educators agree that relationships are necessary for student academic success. Most have heard about or read at least some of the research that confirms this connection. But, for many, it isn't easy to develop these relationships. Teachers want good relationships with their students but have some trepidations about the idea. Some aren't sure exactly what those relationships could or should be. Others fear that they don't have the right personality to establish meaningful, warm relationships with students. Some think that time spent building relationships robs time from their content areas. Some are concerned about transitioning from community time to the more structured academic time. Many admit (and many more feel it but don't admit it) that they just don't know how to do this.

This chapter is here—right near the beginning of the book—to offer help. I want to help you understand why this is so important, what real teachers have experienced, what research confirms about student-teacher relationships and classroom management, and what difference this makes for students. The chapter will show you what trusting, positive student–teacher relationships look like and how to grow and nurture them. In addition, you'll find a selection of specific strategies you can use to start building relationships that matter.

Why Relationships Matter

Let's start with the bottom line—what teachers know without consulting any research: If students don't like you or don't feel you like them, they are not going to like being in your class, and they are not going to work hard. Students can't learn if they feel scared, desperately alone, invisible, unvalued, unknown. If students feel cared for, valued, and important—if they feel you are genuinely interested in them—they will feel safe enough to learn and grow.

Trust is the key ingredient in efforts to raise standards and improve student learning and achievement.

There is a growing body of exciting and fascinating research that gives us insight into why and how student-teacher relationships make a difference. Here are a few of the key findings. (I hope you can find time to dig deeper into some of the sources mentioned. You'll find full citations at the end of the book.)

- Teachers who develop personal relationships with students experience **fewer behavioral problems** in the classroom and see **better academic performance** in their students. Positive student–teacher relations are also associated with **liking school more** and with **greater self-direction** by students (Decker, Dona, & Christenson, 2007; Haberman, 1995; Marzano & Marzano, 2003; Goodenow, 1993).

- Teachers' actions in their classrooms have **twice as much impact** on student achievement as assessment policies, community involvement, or staff collegiality. Teachers who have high-quality relationships with students have **significantly fewer discipline problems, rule violations,** and **other related problems** in class over a year's time than teachers who do not (Marzano & Marzano, 2003).

- Student–teacher connectedness has a **buffering effect in the presence of bullying** that can otherwise negatively affect achievement (Konishi, et al., 2007).

- Students' **academic success** is optimized within caring, supportive, safe environments. A caring school environment is associated with **higher grades, greater student engagement, higher expectations, better attendance, and fewer discipline problems** (Goodenow, 1993; Patrick, Hicks, & Ryan, 1997; Hymel, et al., 2006; Luiselli, et al., 2005; Zins, et al., 2004; McCombs, 2004; Schaps, et al., 2004).

- Student perceptions of teacher support are associated with **greater feelings of belonging**, greater academic engagement and motivation, greater valuing of academic subjects, higher expectations for academic success, and better academic performance. **They are a stronger predictor of school interest** than perceived parent or peer support (Birch & Ladd, 1998; Wentzel, 1997; Wentzel, 1998).

- **Trust is the key ingredient** in efforts to raise standards and improve student learning and achievement. A school can have abundant resources and effective teaching programs in place, but student learning will suffer if trusting student-teacher relationships are not part of the formula. "Strong, trusting student–teacher relationships are essential for learning" (Bryk and Schneider, 2002, pg 31).

- When students perceive support within their school environment and feel respected and valued, they have **fewer feelings of loneliness and less depression and anxiety** (Juvonen, Nishina, & Graham, 2000).

If You Can't Manage Them . . .

- Students who perceive their teachers as caring **engage more with academic content**, take intellectual risks, adapt their behavior more appropriately, and keep trying in the face of failure. At middle school and high school levels, students are more likely to be engaged with their learning, and in high school, are **less likely to drop out** (Davis, 2006).

- Students in middle grades are more likely to experience declines in academic motivation and self-esteem than students in other grade spans. These **declines can be linked to the classroom**—particularly to unsatisfactory student-teacher relationships (Adler, 2002; Anderman, Maehr, & Midgley, 1999; Furrer & Skinner, 2003).

I'VE GOT THIS COOL NEW TEACHER FOR MATH CLASS. MAYBE I WON'T DROP OUT AFTER ALL.

I share these research outcomes with you because I know they are true! I have seen and experienced all of these. Believe me, you will never regret time you spend getting to know your students and working at strong, empathetic relationships. This time will pay off ten-fold because you will spend much LESS time on that other painful, unproductive stuff, such as wrangling with students, handling discipline issues, and bouncing back from disruptions to valuable learning experiences. Don't underestimate the power of relationships in your classroom. As Ron Wolk, educator and founding editor of *Education Week* has said, "For many teachers, relationships ARE their teaching" (2003, pg 14).

What Good Relationships Look Like

So far, I've used a variety of words to describe relationships: *good, effective, caring, trusting, empathetic, high-quality, positive, connective*—and all these are apt adjectives. Taken all together (and DO take them all together), I am sure you get the drift. One critical word in the list of descriptors is *effective*. The kinds of relationships I am talking about here **WORK** to help adolescents thrive and grow personally, socially, emotionally, and academically. That's the goal of our chosen profession! That's what we intend to do!

> For many teachers, relationships ARE their teaching.
> –Ron Wolk

To be more specific, here are some signs that trusting, caring student-teacher relationships are present in a classroom. Look for these. Cultivate these.

- The teacher pays attention to students—as individuals.
- Students feel noticed. They do not look scared or alienated.
- Students have a voice. Their opinions are invited.
- The teacher listens (and responds) to students.
- Students are accepted. Their demeanor shows that they feel safe.
- The teacher speaks to students respectfully.
- The teacher does not yell.
- The teacher does not label, judge, or belittle students.
- The teacher's body language projects acceptance and care.
- The teacher respects the students' privacy.
- Students look comfortable in the presence of the teacher.

If You Can't Manage Them . . .

- The teacher does not speak sarcastically.
- There are no signs that the teacher favors some students over others.
- The teacher's actions show that he or she understands well the characteristics and needs of the age group.
- Students' talents, opinions, interests, and accomplishments are honored and celebrated.
- The teacher does not discipline, scold, or chide a student in front of other students.
- There are no signs of phoniness in the teacher.
- The teacher treats all students with respect at all times.
- It is evident that the teacher takes a personal interest in each student beyond his or her classroom performance or behavior.
- The teacher builds activities that ensure success for all students.
- The teacher models fair, respectful, positive behaviors.
- The teacher's behavior shows that he or she knows the academic talents, needs, and struggles of each student.

How to Nurture Relationships

As I wrote earlier in the chapter, many teachers aren't confident that they can pull off these relationships. Teachers that I mentor, or teachers I meet when I do presentations at conferences, will often say something like this: "But Kim, you have this natural ability to relate to kids. You're comfortable with them. You're fun and funny and straightforward. YOU can do this. But I don't have your personality."

So let me say this right now: **You don't have to be Kim Campbell to build successful relationships with kids.** You don't have to be a crack-up, a comedian, laid back, easygoing, or a wild extrovert! And I have research to back me up! Studies show something that should encourage you: Characteristics of effective student-teacher relationships are not dependent upon the teacher's personality. They are not even related to whether or not the teacher is a favorite of the students! Instead, effective relationships are characterized by specific behaviors, strategies, and fundamental attitudes that the teacher demonstrates (Rogers & Renard, 1999; Bender, 2003; Hall & Hall, 2003; Wolk, 2003).

Effective student–teacher relationships are not dependent on the teacher's personality.

This is good news! If you're one of those who is nervous about establishing caring, trusting relationships with students—listen up! You can learn to do this! Review Chapter 1 if you want to examine the fundamental attitudes that can help you become (or keep you from being) a good manager. This chapter has already mentioned some specific behaviors, and here are more:

Good student-teacher relationships grow in the classroom when you . . .

1. believe in students and help them believe in themselves.

2. understand the developmental characteristics and needs of the age group, and show this in your actions.

3. get to know each student as a learner—her abilities, his strengths, her struggles, his learning style, her fears.

If You Can't Manage Them . . .

4. help students identify and develop their own unique abilities.

5. help students succeed academically; help a student master something with which she or he has struggled.

6. nurture their abilities to help themselves.

7. help students polish social skills they need to belong in class and wider social circles.

8. help students develop skills of self-control, cooperation, adaptability, and judgment.

9. help students develop decision-making and problem-solving skills.

10. help them successfully navigate the pitfalls, difficulties, "hidden" rules, and "red tape" of middle school or high school.

11. get to know personal stuff about each student—experiences, abilities, interests, activities, worries.

12. set clear expectations and help students reach them.

Notice that "fundamental attitudes that the teacher demonstrates" is one of the cornerstones of student-teacher relationships (see page 33). I wrote about this in Chapter 1, but will repeat it here: What you believe (or fear) about your students, about yourself, about learning, and about the teaching process—will affect the manager you become when you set foot in the classroom. This will also affect your relationships with students.

Students' perceptions of your underlying attitudes—and thus students' relationships with you—are constantly affected by . . .

- how you speak to them (including tone of voice)
- your authenticity

- differences in how you speak to them when another adult is present versus when no other adults are present
- your body language
- your facial expressions
- your boundaries (or lack thereof)
- your expression of your own emotions
- ways you show you care (or don't care)

Caring—One Student at a Time

Care keeps showing up in this chapter. So much of the research about positive relationships includes this word. The idea gets tossed around a lot. But how, specifically, do you show you care? **First of all, you can't just talk about caring. You have to REALLY care.** Students—particularly adolescents—can spot a phony miles away. They hear a lot of caring talk. And believe me, they know the authentic thing when they hear it.

I add the word *empathy* to the discussion of caring because this is the kind of care needed to build effective relationships. Many research studies confirm that **empathy on the part of a helper is the most important component in a relationship that really helps someone**—and this is particularly true for difficult adolescents (Goldfried, Greenberg, & Marmar, 1990; Mordock, 1991; Garfield, 1994; Orlinsky, Grawe, & Parks, 1994; Sexton & Whiston, 1994; Bernstein, 1996; Hanna, Hanna, & Keys, 1999).

Back in 1956, psychologist Alfred Adler defined empathy as "seeing with the eyes of another, hearing with the ears of another, and feeling with the heart of another" (pg 135). Empathy goes way beyond saying you care. It goes way beyond being kind and respectful. This is caring at a personal level. Showing students that you value their interests, cultures, and life experiences helps foster healthy relationships with them.

When teachers ask me how to show empathy, I find the answer easy: "Begin by establishing authentic, personal relationships—one student at a time." This is how you demonstrate caring—by being interested in each student as a person.

How to let students know you are interested?
Here are some general principles:

TALK! Open a two-way dialogue. Ask questions. Ask for their opinions and insights.

LISTEN. Ask meaningful questions and listen to the students' answers. Ask for feedback. Pay attention to what they say. Listen actively. Respond encouragingly without judgment.

LEARN. Find out about their interests, fears, activities, joys, family, out-of-school lives. Learn their stories.

RELAX. Do not micromanage the dialogue. Let them have the first word. Let them have the last word.

ENGAGE. Engage them on their learning. Get to know how they are working, what they need, what is easy, what is hard.

REMEMBER. Revisit topics and conversations to show that you remember the students' activities, goals, and interests.

NURTURE REFLECTION. Ask lots of reflective questions. Provide your students with ways to evaluate their experiences and reflect on their questions, discoveries, and accomplishments.

SHARE. Tell the students something about yourself—your interests, outside-school experiences, family, mishaps, and goals.

This might sound hard. It might sound time-consuming. You might doubt that it is worth it. So I will end with three reminders.

One

Hard? Maybe, but since when do we want to avoid "hard"? Hey, we're teachers! We work our XXXXX's off! We can do hard! But here's the thing: Students perceive their teachers as caring **when they make attempts** to understand and connect with their students as individuals. Reread those bold words above. Students—even adolescents—are bigger-hearted than they show. For all their tough exteriors, and despite their great skills at disguising their feelings, they crave positive, meaningful interaction with adults. They will see any genuine attempts you make, and they will respond.

Furthermore, this relationship thing—it not only helps students. As you develop positive personal relationships with students, YOU will be nurtured. You will find more joy in teaching. And you will not feel this is so hard.

> Students can't learn if they feel desperately alone—invisible, unvalued, unknown.

If You Can't Manage Them . . .

Two

Time-consuming? You bet! But isn't this what you spend your time doing anyway? Relating to students? You WILL have relationships with students. You already do. The question is—will they be contentious? Unsatisfying? Disruptive to learning? Or will they be positive and growth-producing for students and for you?

Furthermore, many of the techniques you can use do not take up a lot of time. There are dozens of ways to show personal interest with a brief question, comment, walk down the hall, short note, or 30-second chat. Whatever time it takes will pay off in rewards not measurable in minutes and time **not** wasted on management issues.

Three

Worth it? Absolutely. I can't say this enough (as you have probably noticed). Student engagement is connected to the feeling that he matters, that she is valued. Students will feel safer. They will behave better. They will be more engaged in learning. They will achieve at higher levels.

Furthermore, YOU will change forever as a classroom manager. You've seen the research and read about benefits. These are not theoretical. They are for real.

Relationship-Building Strategies

Every teacher needs a toolbox full of ideas and activities for building relationships with her or his students. Here are several of my favorites. And be prepared! As you put strategies like these to work, your confidence as a classroom manager will bloom along with good relationships.

If It Works, Keep Doing It

I would guess that you already have some good techniques for building relationships with students. So this is the best place to start. Try to identify them. Go back to the reflection you did at the beginning of this chapter (*I've Got Relationships, Right?*). You wrote down some things you know about each student in one of your classes. Think about how you came to know these things. What strategies have you used to make personal connections with individual students? Make a list of approaches, questions, or behaviors that you already use to build relationships. Then keep doing what you know works. Expand those tactics to other students. Add more strategies and goals to your list as your year progresses.

The Greeting that Keeps on Giving

Greeting anyone, especially students, is the initial step in the beginning of any relationship. I mean greeting them with something other than, "Please take your seats and quiet down," or "Turn to page 23 and let's get started." Students need to feel welcomed. They need to feel your interest in them.

I start each of my classes by saying, "Hi, Team!" Students greet me with a greeting they have chosen. Early in the year, students make recommendations. The class decides with a vote. Over the years, I have had various types of greetings—everything from a grunt to a line from the sitcom *Friends*: "How you doin'?" Whatever the choice, I greet the students and they greet me before we start class.

If You Can't Manage Them . . .

"Hi, Team!" is a deliberate choice for me. I use this greeting because in essence I am attempting to create a team atmosphere within my classroom. My years as a coach taught me the value of establishing a team concept in the classroom. A team works together, helps each other succeed, and is led by a motivated coach. A coach inspires, teaches, disciplines, and clearly recognizes the importance of building relationships with the athletes to access their full potential. Teachers who use a coach's mentality, both as an instructor and a disciplinarian, may see great benefits in student response and behavior.

It never fails; every year I will have a student ask me, "Why do you start class with 'Hi, team'?" Oh, the joys of those teachable moments! Once this question is asked, I have the opportunity to explain how important it is for all students in this class to function as a team, to work together, to understand that there is no "I" in team—all that good stuff that coaches do and say every day.

Greet, Meet, Manage

A great way to make sure you connect with each student is to hand out materials (index cards, worksheets, and so on) as they enter the classroom. This allows you to greet each student, connecting with each on a personal level—asking a short question, or giving a short comment or encouragement. Since hall duty is usually part of every teacher's job, greeting students in the hallway or at the door works well to help the students begin to focus on your class and subject area. Many teachers dread transitions because of management problems. A nice bonus of "greet, meet, and manage" is that it cuts out a transition. (Make sure that whatever you hand them is something they can begin without your help and not something they can copy from each other.)

With some classes, standing in the hall handing out materials is simply asking for trouble. I'm thinking of a class I had with 25 boys and four girls. Once the boys entered the class, the room became a football field. They would push, shove, and toss whatever was not fastened down; therefore, I had to begin managing even before the class officially began. My solution still involved greeting everyone at the door and handing out necessary materials, but I stood partially in the doorway so my eyes could take in both my room and the hallway. Hey, it worked—the football game ended with my WHOLE team winning!

Share, Talk, Bond

Following our daily group greeting, I ask my students if they have anything they want to share with the class and me today. This invites students to share appropriate comments and stories; it allows me to learn about their lives outside of the classroom. And, maybe just as importantly, it gives me a chance to share appropriate stories about myself (such as tales about the dog I love so much, and so on). This models sharing and trust, and gives students a glimpse of me as a person and not just a teacher.

If You Can't Manage Them . . .

As a part of the sharing time, I can help students learn to set and stay within boundaries. We have time boundaries—limits on how long each person can talk and a time limit for the sharing period. We also have guidelines for what is appropriate to share, and for ways to listen respectfully and tolerantly.

Students share personal details such as their ball game scores or the birth of a baby sister or the latest favorite popular song. Share time builds an atmosphere of inclusion, relaxation, and safety. Placing a strict time limit on daily sharing helps students know when it's time to start class work.

As students feel comfortable, they often feel safe enough to share very personal things. One of my students shared about sexual molestation by her sister's boyfriend. The class grew silent—looking at me. I stood there, heart pounding, wondering what to say. I responded simply, "I am so sorry to hear that. I appreciate your sharing. Perhaps when things like this happen, we could share them in private or with the school counselor. Also, I hope all of you realize that I must tell the authorities about this. It's a law I have to follow as a teacher."

She looked at me and said, "Ya, I know." After class I held the student back and we talked again. I explained in detail why I had to report this to the counselor. My heart tells me she knew this and it could be why she shared. So, remember as you build strong, positive relationships, students will start to open up to you and share things that may place you in an uncomfortable position. The benefits of developing those relationships will be worth all the uncomfortable moments you experience.

Share time has become such a part of my classroom and routine that when it doesn't happen, my students seem to be out of sorts. They don't function as well. For example, I had a class with 25 boys and four girls. (Yes, we all survived.) Every time I had to be gone, this particular class would give the substitute teacher fits. And every time I would come back, we would talk about it and try to figure out why their behavior was so awful. Finally, one student said, "Ms. C, I think I know why we struggle when you are gone. It's because the sub never lets us have share time. The day just gets off to a bad start."

Don't worry—time spent creating a safe environment and enjoyment of each other will make your academic time more productive. BUT, if you want to shorten the time, try one of these:

> Teachers need to know what is going on at home for us— what might affect our actions in and out of school.
>
> – Brenden, grade 7

1. As students do an academic warm-up activity at their seats, walk around and talk to students about things that do not relate to school.

2. Take a quick break in the middle of class. Stop, drop, and share. Take five minutes to just let them share highlights of their day or week with a partner or with the class.

3. Do share time at the end of the class period, when you have those last five minutes that seem to be wasted and the students are just milling around waiting to leave.

If You Can't Manage Them . . .

4. For a brief warm-up plus share time, ask students to write on a note card five things that are going well for them this week. Then collect the cards and read a few aloud to the class (with permission). See if other students can guess whose highlight or card you are reading.

Walk & Talk

With so little time and so much to do, teachers have taken multi-tasking to another level. "Walk & Talk" is one way to build or rebuild relationships with your students while you are doing other things you need to do. You can be on hall duty and thinking about your next class. Now, at the same time, you see a student of yours walking in the hallway. You may not have had much time with this student today or for a while, so you begin to walk with this student. The conversation can be light, or it can be about your class, or it can be about anything that relates to this student. You don't have to walk far; you don't have to impart wisdom. "Walk & Talk" simply means that you visit with students as you walk and build your relationship as you talk.

Writing Your Life

Few things are so connecting as telling one's story to someone else who cares enough to read or listen. Take some time early in the year for students to write an autobiography or create some other piece of writing that tells some part of a life story. Share whatever pieces of this writing that students grant permission to share. Find a way to publish parts of these—again with student permission. This process will deepen your understanding of individuals and also help students know and appreciate one another.

You're the First to Know

We all know how important it is to be in contact with parents on a regular basis, and how critical it is to build good relationships with parents. We also know that we need to be aware of how our contact with parents may affect the child–parent relationship as well as our relationship with the child. But remember that, as the teacher, **your primary relationship is with the student**. Parents are second. So, when incidents happen between you and a student, it is vitally important that you do **not** call home to inform the parents unless you have told the student you would do so. Of course, there are exceptions to this, but informing the student first helps maintain trust between you and the student.

By informing the student, you model problem-solving behavior and honest open communication. You also model respect—you do not report to the student's authority figures before informing the student. I have no reservations about calling parents when there is a need; in fact, a relationship with parents is my second most important relationship. I simply inform the student before calling the parent. Remember, the bottom line is that you and the student will see each other every day, and you need to find a way to make things work between the two of you. When a need arises to visit with a parent in a disciplinary action or academic concern, I will inform the student before contacting the parent, unless there is an emergency or an extraordinary circumstance.

Informing the student first helps maintain trust between you and the student.

Each year our school has an Open House. I use this opportunity to explain my philosophy to my parents. I also tell them that when I **do** call, I need their help. I will likely be calling because I have exhausted all of my ideas for working with their child. The number of affirmative nods I see in my audience of parents tells me that this philosophy resonates with them.

● ● ● ● You Gotta Know When to Hold 'Em, Know When to Scold 'Em

Most adolescents want to be liked. That includes being liked and respected by their teachers. However, teachers of adolescents know they will often do or say something that requires teachers to redirect, discipline, or remove them from the classroom. Neither the teacher nor the student enjoys this experience. The problem might be a power struggle; it could be an infraction of classroom rules; or it might be just plain misbehavior. You must handle these situations with firmness, with the understood consequences for the infraction. At the same time, you must deal with the anger (yours and the student's). When these situations happen, you, as an adult, can move on fairly easily. You can usually be somewhat objective about the incident. Students, however, may not be capable of or willing to see the whole picture.

All too often, what does **not** happen is the follow-up or check-in between teacher and student after the incident. Sometimes the teacher and the student don't see each other until the child arrives back at class the next day. The student has spent approximately 24 hours wondering if the teacher is still angry, if the teacher is ready to move on, or if the teacher will hold a grudge for the rest of the year. She or he may hold onto the anger, feeling wronged and embarrassed. For the adolescent brain, this spells concern and possible trouble. For some adolescents, this situation turns into a power struggle and they will arrive at class ready to win at all costs. Insecurity may lead them to act out again, try to get your attention inappropriately, or even skip class. Students often form opinions and develop attitudes that can be hard to change. For some adolescents, the brain tells them to quit, to give up; that it's not worth the effort or worth attending class. In addition, the student may feel that the classroom is no longer a safe place.

Therefore, I never let my "watch" end without connecting with a student whom I've had to discipline in class. Whenever I have had a significant situation with a student (such as removal from class), I always take time to find the student during the school day. I reconnect with her or him by "walking and talking," taking my prep time to find the student and visit about the incident, or finding him or her after school (or at least before school or class the next day). I approach the student with a greeting and quickly tell him or her that I think we need to talk about what happened, and I ask if the student agrees. If the answer is no, I express that I need to talk about it. If the answer is yes, I ask if the student wants to give a viewpoint or explanation first—or should I? We then proceed to talk about what happened in a manner that helps us understand each other better. This gives the student a chance to be heard or to apologize, and it gives me a chance to let the student know what that kind of behavior does to the class, to the student, and to me. This type of discussion leads to understanding, trust, and respect between us.

Take this time to check in or touch base after a problem. For me, this has rebuilt and saved countless relationships with kids. It has also made me a better teacher because I hear and listen to their perspectives when both of us are calm. It is my responsibility as the teacher and as the adult to talk to that student about my feelings, my actions, his or her feelings, and his or her actions. If you work with preadolescents and adolescents, you will probably have to scold them, but you also need to "hold" them (respect their thoughts and feelings in order to maintain and preserve that relationship). Yes, it takes extra time, effort, and courage, but the benefits and modeling of connective behavior are well worth it.

> A teacher who cares about me is always there when I need her.
> – Shayla, grade 8

"Sorry" Seems So Hard to Say

Teachers are human. We experience lots of emotions. When working in a middle or high school, those emotions can present themselves in a variety of ways and at a variety of times. Sometimes when incidents with students have an emotional impact on us, we don't always respond and react in the best way possible. After all, regardless of what they say, we *are* human. Instead of waiting, calming down, and making a decision or a comment when we are less fired up (or hurt), we may respond or make a decision out of an immediate reaction. Even a headache or just being tired can lead to an overreaction.

One thing I've learned in working with adolescent students is that it is okay to admit that you, the teacher, are wrong. I have apologized to students in private as well as to the entire class. When I do admit to being wrong, my credibility does not weaken; rather it is strengthened because I have accepted responsibility for my part in an unfortunate situation. I have modeled accepting responsibility by saying two words: "I'm sorry." I truly believe that the more human qualities I can reveal and use, the more I "teach" and the more I will create an environment of trust, safety, and cooperation.

Shake It Up Baby, Now

About three weeks into my school year, I introduce my students to the special secret Campbell Handshake. I make a big deal about how lucky I am to have the best students in our school, and that I think the time has come for all of us to have a secret handshake, only to be shared with fellow Campbell kids. It's a small way to make my students feel special and to build community. I use the Campbell Handshake to break up a long sitting period in class. I'll say something such as, "Okay, we've been quiet and sitting too long. Find a partner and give that person the Campbell Shake." I also use the shake during transition times or to greet their work groups. Whenever we have a guest in our class, the class insists on teaching the secret shake. The handshake has evolved over the years as each class adds a new part. Caution: If you plan to do this in your classroom and you know you have a gang presence in your school, talk to your police liaison or school counselor so you are aware of gang hand gestures.

THE SECRET HANDSHAKE: LIKE THIS!

● ● ● ● Pictures Are Worth 1,000 Words

Today's generation of students are referred to as "digital natives" and veteran teachers as "digital immigrants" (Prensky, 2010). Technology is the language of your students. And we miss opportunities to connect with students if we have little interest in, few good ways to effectively use, or little experience with tools of technology. Look for opportunities to incorporate technology into your teaching and classroom life. Look for opportunities to use these tools to deepen connections.

Use digital presentation programs and such tools as active boards (interactive digital white boards) to project visuals that will help students grasp concepts. Add a personal touch by interjecting pictures of yourself or your interests. After a recent trip to China, I shared pictures of my experience. To break up the routine, and to see if students were paying attention, I had added among the slides a picture of myself at my high school prom. So, here we were cruising along on a lesson about China, when suddenly there appeared a picture of my date and me 20 years ago. After the laughter and a short discussion on how I was able to get my hair to stand up that tall, we returned to our discussion on China. (Beware! I had one student actually ask me if I really did wear that outfit to China. I let him ponder that one for a while.)

The Laughter Connection

Try this: Survey your students about characteristics that make an effective teacher. I guarantee that "fun" will show up on most lists. One year I surveyed my students and asked them the following question: "Many of you like 'fun' teachers. What does it mean to be a fun teacher?" The most consistent answer given was that a fun teacher is someone who laughs and smiles.

Unfortunately, I have heard countless teachers say, "Well, I'm just not a funny person; never have been and never will be." After watching some of them teach, I am in total agreement with their diagnoses! However, what the surveyed students said was that **a fun teacher is**

someone who laughs and smiles. They did not say, "A fun teacher is one who is funny" or "A fun teacher is one who makes us laugh." I believe what students are saying is that they relate to teachers who have a sense of humor, teachers who smile, teachers who laugh with their students, and teachers who laugh at themselves. This is not the same as being a funny teacher.

Laughter and humor are connective. When you show your sense of humor, you show that you are human—especially if students see that you can laugh at yourself. Laughter breaks barriers of age and ability. It can defuse tense situations. When you smile, you show students that you are happy being around them. When you laugh, you show students that you enjoy sharing something funny with them. This is especially important if you are trying to develop relationships with adolescents. Humor helps students relax and enjoy each other, too.

> Humor is a wonderful connector. But sarcasm has no place in a classroom.

Let me caution you, though. Humor is only connective when it is appropriate and when it is not harmful. You will find more about humor and classroom management in Chapter 11, but I emphasize here that a teacher must *never* laugh at a student or participate in laughing or smiling when someone else is criticizing or teasing a student. Sarcasm is not appropriate humor for a classroom. Humor is a wonderful connector. But sarcasm has no place in a classroom—even with teenagers.

Find Out What You Don't Know

As teachers, we all hope that every child in the school has a trusting relationship with some adult in the school community. We recognize that many students, particularly those who are shy and quiet, do what they are supposed to do, and may fly under the relationship radar. It is critical that we have strategies—alone, and particularly together with colleagues or teammates—to get a true picture of students' connections to adults. We must find out which students are falling through the cracks.

One way to do this is to join together for an activity known as the Student Name Game. Before you start, your group of adults must discuss and agree on what constitutes a relationship. (My team of teachers decided that a relationship consisted of knowing something personal about a student other than how they perform or behave in class.) Also before you start, understand that this is not a competition among teachers, nor will the activity involve any judgment of their relationship-building skills. This is purely about the students—a genuine effort to see that every student has at least one safe, trusted adult ally in the school.

Note that this is an extension of the activity you did on page 24. What is different here is that this is done with a team or group of teachers who deal with the same students, and the goal is to find students who have fallen through the cracks.

1. At a team, department, or faculty meeting, place the name of each student on your team (or in your school/

grade/department) on an index card. Sit in a circle. Distribute the cards evenly among the teachers.

2. Each teacher pulls out of his or her stack the name cards of students with whom they have a relationship— then passes the remaining cards to the left. Repeat the process until all teachers have viewed all cards.

3. Take the remaining name cards and spread them out on the floor, table, or cork board.

4. Each teacher then "adopts" one or two (or more, depending on the number of teachers and students) of the remaining students.

5. Each teacher sets a plan to connect with the students they adopted. This works best if teachers set goals in writing, identify strategies, and keep track of their contacts with the students.

6. This is a powerful way to make the topic of relationships concrete and personal. Come back together as a group in a month and repeat the activity. Share the techniques you have used. Share stories about these students to see how this approach has affected them.

● ● ● ● Trust Busters

In his book *Teach Like Your Hair's On Fire* (2007), Rafe Esquith says that students must be able to trust that you are in charge, that you will keep them safe, and that respect will be mutual. He also says trust is so important that you need to talk to students about it during the first two minutes of the first day of class. Not only must teachers talk about trust, they must also demonstrate trust, either by reading a story or devising a specific activity.

Developing trust is critical in any relationship. Teachers model trust and trustworthiness (or lack of these) every day. Do you follow through with what you say you are going to do? If you say you are going to give the students a break during class, do you? Do you tell your students that you will return their tests tomorrow . . . then don't? Do you threaten to send a student to the hallway for their behavior . . . then don't? These are just a few examples of trust busters that can damage your relationships with students.

Students are watching you all the time and deciding if you can be trusted. Don't let them down.

It's a great compliment when students ask you to attend a sporting event or concert, but never tell them you are going to be there when you know you have other commitments. Be honest and simply tell them you have other responsibilities and can't make it. Middle and high school students can clearly understand when you tell them you are busy versus your simply not showing up when you said you would. Students are watching you all the time and deciding if you can be trusted. Don't let them down.

What's Up?

If you are going to connect with kids, you just *have to* know what's going on with them. I've already written about individual connection. Here, I mean—know what they are liking, mimicking, listening to, dancing to, singing, watching, carrying around, wearing. Get with it!

If You Can't Manage Them . . .

Learn their language. (You don't have to use it, just know what it means.) Get familiar with their music and jargon. Watch some of the TV shows, YouTube hits, and other media stuff that captivates them. Know how the social networks work. Know how to read the text messages you see. Surprise them! They might think they can talk about stuff that you'd never get. Burst out into lyrics of a hit song (appropriate lyrics, of course). Get familiar with the technology they use. Don't get buried in the sand. Keep up so you know what's up!

Move Slowly

No matter what student-teacher relationship strategy you create or borrow, be sure to start with low-risk activities. Take small steps toward your goal of building relationships. Don't push students to uncomfortable or false connections. By mid-year you probably will be ready to take bigger risks with your students. And they'll be ready to risk more connection.

> When the students know you care, it changes everything— the way they see you, themselves, and their whole school experience.
> – Maurine, high school parent

Never underestimate the effects of positive relationships with students. I'll risk repeating my message of this entire chapter: Great teachers purposely and consistently conduct relationship-building activities inside and outside their classrooms. This will make all the other techniques in the rest of this book come to you more easily.

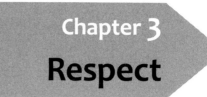

You've gotta give it to get it.

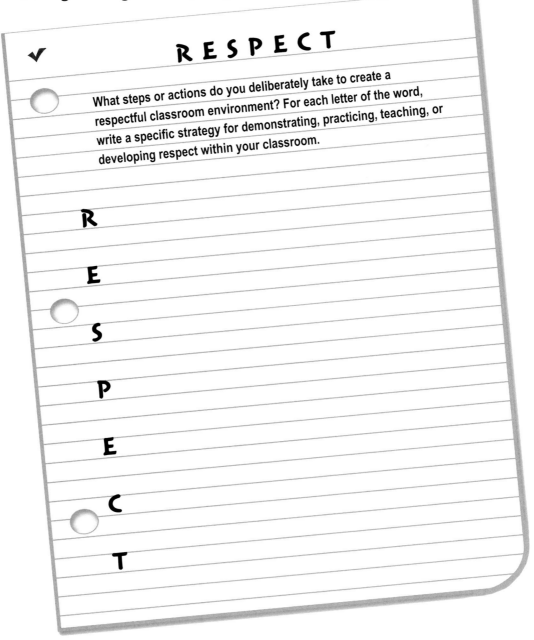

R E S P E C T

✔

What steps or actions do you deliberately take to create a respectful classroom environment? For each letter of the word, write a specific strategy for demonstrating, practicing, teaching, or developing respect within your classroom.

R

E

S

P

E

C

T

I feel respected when I know
    the teacher recognizes me. — Jasmine

I feel respected when the teacher
    tries to understand my issues. — Sean P.

I feel respected when I get called on
    and complimented. — Khalil S.

I feel disrespected when someone
    treats me as less than I am. — Blake B.

I feel respected when
    I'm being acknowledged. — Ike

I feel respected when people
    look at me while I am talking. — Jayden

I feel disrespected when the teacher
    yells at me but no one else. — Gabby O.

I feel respected when I'm trusted
    to do something. — Timothy S.

I feel respected when a teacher
    remembers stuff about me. — Zoey B.

I feel disrespected when a teacher
    doesn't take students' ideas seriously. — Bit K.

I feel respected when the teacher
    asks how we are doing in life. — Quintasia J.

I feel respected when a teacher
    recognizes my best efforts. — Greta W.

R.E.S.P.E.C.T.! Aretha Franklin sings about it. Lots of comedians (and plenty of the rest of us) complain that they never get any. We all need it. Everybody (not just someone with the "teacher" or "adult" label) deserves it. These seventh-grade speakers know exactly what it feels like (and what the opposite feels like). And a commitment to it is part of just about every list of classroom rules. In some classrooms, it is the only rule!

If You Can't Manage Them . . .

The word *respect* inevitably enters the conversation on that first day of school when teachers discuss rules. I can hear myself now—saying, "One of my expectations is that we respect each other." (I can hear myself adding the idea of respecting each other's opinions and differences.) After several years of this approach, I realized I was operating under the (faulty) assumption that students understood exactly what I meant. Teachers continually demand respect. But students do not always know exactly what it means or what it looks like in a classroom.

> **Don't make this assumption.** Students receive all kinds of media messages that show disrespect at every turn (reality shows, commercials with offensive humor, celebrities who say whatever comes to mind no matter the content or possible harm to others, ads, music videos, YouTube videos, and dozens of images that illustrate disrespect for individuals, women, or particular groups). According to a 2010 Kaiser Family Foundation report, 8- to 18-year-olds spend over seven hours a day using entertainment media. This does not count time doing homework (Rideout, Foehr, & Roberts, 2010). The more students see and hear disrespect, the more desensitized they become to it. It is no wonder that they feel it's okay to treat peers and adults with disrespect.

Teachers must deliberately explain, discuss, and nurture respect so students know when it is present and when it is not. Teachers must deliberately confront disrespect. Without respect, the satisfactory student-teacher relationships and safety needed for optimal learning cannot exist. Respect is a cornerstone for effective classroom management. But it is not something that happens because you make it a rule. It has to be modeled, taught, and consistently examined. Disrespect must also be examined and discussed.

What Is Respect?

Respect yourself and you will respect others.
– Confucius

The word *respect* comes from the Latin word *respectare*, which means *to look again*. At its deepest level, it means *seeing another person*. This kind of seeing involves acknowledging a person as a fellow human being worthy of esteem. One formal definition of respect is *a feeling of esteem for a person or other entity and specific actions that show esteem*. Other definitions use such words and phrases as:

> *to take notice of,*
> *to admire,*
> *to show regard for,*
> *to regard with special attention,* or
> *to treat as consequential.*

Do not confuse respect with tolerance. Tolerance does not imply any positive feeling. Respect is a positive stance. Respect is characterized by actions that honor somebody. Any mutually satisfying relationship is based on each person noticing and honoring the other. Do not confuse respect with obedience. Students might obey you, but that could be out of fear. It does not mean they respect you.

Sometimes it is helpful to understand a concept by looking at its opposite. The opposite of respect is *scorn* or *contempt*—regarding a person or group as inferior or worthless. Contempt is usually directed at someone perceived as having lower status than oneself. It manifests itself as disgust or disregard. You can be alerted to the absence of respect when you see any signs of contempt, disgust, or scorn.

The Chain of Respect

Respect is a powerful management tool for promoting a classroom climate where students can learn and grow academically, socially, personally, and emotionally. But, as I said before, this is not a simple matter of **requiring** respect. Development of a respectful classroom takes skill, dedication, and a whole lot of teaching.

"Classroom management" in the sense of making your life easier or getting kids to behave better is **not** the best motivation for working on respect. The reasons for practicing respect among persons in your classroom are more important than just fewer discipline problems. You **will** have fewer discipline problems—but that is not the main goal. The reason for focusing on respect is that all human beings need it and deserve it. Feeling respected and being able to give respect contribute to a satisfying, successful life. Disrespect is highly damaging—both to the person who is disrespected and the one who does the disrespecting. Each of your students needs to feel respect and give respect to others— for their self-preservation, happiness, learning, and life!

The chain of respect starts with you. If you (the adult in the room, the leader) do not demonstrate respect, it is not likely to happen in your classroom. So here's the chain:

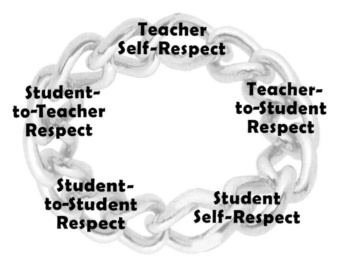

And note that this chain is a circle—the respect that starts with you will come back to you.

Teacher Self-Respect

Respect in your classroom begins **within** you—with your own respect for yourself. Self-respect is about feeling valued. It's about loving yourself for who you are. Your sense of value begins at birth and is shaped throughout childhood. Many incidents and people add to the sense of self that begins in the home. If a child is treated with love and esteem for his or her real self, the chances for healthy self-respect will be good. Other people affect the development of our esteem for ourselves, but ultimately it comes from within.

It is surprising how many people do not respect themselves. This will take work for those who were not treated with respect, particularly during childhood. But it is important to work on, because a lack of self-respect will get passed on to others around us—in forms that are unhealthful. To begin the chain of respect in your classroom, give some thought to your level of self-respect. Ask yourself questions such as:

- *Do I feel that my opinions are valuable?*
- *Am I true to myself?*
- *Do I present a false self to others?*
- *How do I feel about my abilities as a teacher?*
- *Do I fall apart when I am criticized?*
- *Do I feel good about my appearance?*
- *Am I plagued by jealousy?*
- *Do I frequently feel disdain for others?*
- *Do I bounce back from hard knocks?*
- *Am I able to forgive myself and others?*
- *Am I burdened by regret or guilt?*
- *Do I get caught up in self-destructive behaviors?*
- *Am I glad to be me?*

If you feel that your self-respect is sagging and needs a boost, seek some help to recover it. For out of a secure and healthy respect for yourself, you as a teacher will be able to set off a chain reaction of respect in your classroom!

Teacher-To-Student(s) Respect

It's a given: If you do not respect your students, they will not respect you. And the more disrespect you show, the more disrespect students will return. But the good news is that the opposite is also a given: **Respect from the teacher breeds respect from the students!** This means that you must treat every student with respect all of the time. The message is that simple. Of course, it's not always easy. When students disrespect you, outright challenge you, disrespect one another, or act in ways that frustrate you—you might feel they do not deserve your respect. But that's the thing about respect. **Everyone deserves it all the time.** So, yes, even when a student is being rude, demeaning, or just plain rotten to you—you must treat her or him with respect. It is the only way to build a base of respect in your classroom. Counter disrespect with respect. (Remember, the reason to respect another person is that each person deserves respect— regardless of his or her behavior, attitude, oddities, or personality.)

The esteem (or lack thereof) that you feel in your heart for each student will show in your communications, body language, and responses. Students have great "respect detectors." If there is a hint of disdain, contempt, disregard, scorn, or disgust, the student will sense it, and you can kiss goodbye any hope of a good relationship with that

If You Can't Manage Them . . .

student. And, oh, you can also kiss goodbye effective classroom management!

How can you show that you respect students? Here are a few of the best practices I have observed and used:

1. **Be fair.**

    You do not have to, and often should not, treat all students equally. But you must treat them equitably. Enforce consequences fairly. Do not show favoritism. Be constantly vigilant about this. You will have a tendency to like certain kinds of students or to feel more comfortable with some than others. Fairness demands your commitment to keep those personal preferences in check.

2. **Be positive, affirming, and polite.**

    Encourage and compliment students. Do not embarrass, belittle, or laugh at a student. Give feedback in positive, hopeful terms. Affirm what students are doing right much more than what they are not doing right. Treat students kindly and politely. Say "please" and "thank you." Respect their privacy. This is just good manners!

3. **Be honest.**

    If you misunderstand something or take a wrong action, admit it. Apologize. For some people, admitting they are wrong is akin to cutting off an arm. To admit to being wrong is to look inferior to those around them. I find an appropriate apology to be a wonderful opportunity that generally has positive effects. Admitting you are wrong shows students that you are human. This tells them that, though you are the adult in the room, you do not always know the right answers or make the exactly right choice. When you admit you made a gaffe, the respect you will reap from your students is an immeasurable gain.

4. Listen.

When a student initiates a conversation or responds to something you ask, place yourself at eye level and make eye contact. This shows that you are taking her or him seriously. Make sure you are not attending to the papers in your hand or looking at your watch. Focus your attention to the greatest extent possible on the student. Don't interrupt. After the student has time to convey the message, ask questions that show your interest. Give positive feedback. When the situation involves an issue, incident, or behavior problem, listen to the student's side of the story before jumping to conclusions. Always ask a student to explain what he or she thinks happened. **Let the student talk first** to make his or her case before you make judgments. Don't rush to a decision. Listen and consider the student's points and feelings.

5. Remember and respond.

One of the greatest ways to show respect to your students is to remember what a student tells you about his or her life and then comment on it from time to time. It sounds so simple, but with the responsibilities we have as teachers, it can be difficult to find those times. A little thing, such as mentioning a new sibling or a favorite pastime can be very powerful in showing that you value a student. Many teachers give students a survey at the beginning of the year asking them a variety of personal questions about such things as birthdays, family, and favorite activities. This is a great idea; but the questions and student answers mean nothing if you do not remember and refer to that information now and then. If teachers do not remember and respond, students will come to realize that the survey was only a pretense of interest.

6. Don't yell.

Every kid will tell you that yelling does not work— but worse, it works against you. Kids today will do everything in their power to avoid being "dissed" in front of their peers. If that means taking you on and receiving the ultimate consequence, then they'll risk it. Instead of yelling at them in front of the class or as a class, use "I need" or "this is what needs to happen" or "now is the time to" statements and do everything possible not to raise your voice.

When you raise your voice, you show students that they have succeeded in pushing you to your limit. Basically— if you are yelling, you have lost the battle. You must stay calm, take a breath deep, and be direct and specific about what you want them to do or change. Expect them to do it and they might surprise you and actually do it.

It's hard to hear the respect when someone's yelling.

It's also okay to express utter frustration with your students or with their behavior, and ask them what they can do about it rather than waste everyone's time. When given some power to handle their own classroom behavior, students may actually surprise you again with good ideas about how to improve class behavior. (Be careful! Sometimes students will want to be more directive and authoritative than necessary, giving consequences that are too harsh— even to themselves! It can be fun to say to them, "I wouldn't want to punish any of you that way!")

7. **Watch your body language.**

Because you are the adult, you often have a commanding presence. Take care not to threaten or intimidate students with nonverbal signals. If you stand behind your desk, loom over them, lean into their faces, shake a fist or finger, cross your arms, turn away, heave big disgusted sighs, or back away— you show disrespect. Demonstrate respect with your gestures and body position as well as with your facial expressions, actions, and words.

My good friend and mentor Debbie Silver (also consultant, humorist, and speaker) once gave me this good advice: "When you have to talk to a student about behavior, do not stand directly in front of him. Instead, stand next to him." Debbie believes that this strategy immediately dispels threat, removes the power struggle from the situation, and relaxes everyone involved. I have used this strategy many times and I must say, "It really works!"

8. Confront students in private.

There will be times when you must confront a student about behavior. When confrontation is public, there will be a winner and a loser—at least in the eyes of the student. Make a pledge not to confront students in front of other students. It is much more respectful, and much more effective, to deal with discipline issues or other sensitive issues privately. When you do this in public, you demonstrate disrespect, you lose respect, and the student loses face. When you do it in private, you take away the elements of shame and embarrassment. And you have a chance for connection and reconciliation because the student does not have to put up a defensive front for peers.

> I feel respected when a teacher pulls me over to the side or waits until class is over to tell me I have done something wrong.
> – Sarah, grade 7

It is never a good idea to make an example of a student's behavior. You might think you are teaching the whole class a lesson, but part of the lesson will be disrespect for the student in trouble. And you will lose the chance to teach that student anything.

9. Let them save face.

I learned very early in my career that one way to show respect to students is to always (and I mean always) give students opportunities to save face—to avoid embarrassment in front of their peers. As in #8 above, this is critical in discipline situations. There are many other situations in which this is also necessary. With all those hormones running rampant in preadolescents and adolescents, combined with their intense need for peer acceptance, to lose face could mean to lose everything, including their respect for you. In your career, you will witness eyes tearing up (not just girls but also boys) over the most miniscule things. To adults these situations may seem minor; to students these situations may mean their reputation, their pride, and their position with their peers. For all students—especially boys—you must provide an out. At least temporarily, allow a student to walk away, give her or him a pass to leave the room, and change the subject quickly. These tactics help students redeem themselves in front of the most important people in their lives—peers. If it is a behavior issue or other incident that breaks rules, you must finish the conversation or the confrontation at a later time. All students need to recognize that the teacher respects the need to cry in private, but that tears will not be permission to avoid a discussion about the incident.

10. Be an advocate for students.

This is one of the most powerful strategies you can use to show respect for students. I can remember every detail of a day in sixth grade when my teacher stood up for me. The P.E. teacher came to our homeroom door with a criticism about me. I was fully prepared for humiliation and punishment from the P.E. teacher and my homeroom teacher. Instead, I got a teacher on my side—one who spoke in my defense, asked questions I could not have asked, and helped me state my case. My respect for that teacher soared. So did my confidence in myself.

If You Can't Manage Them . . .

Stand up and speak up for students in tough situations—with parents, or with colleagues. Many students do not experience adults in the school as their advocates. They think of the school setting as "them" (adults) against "us" (students). Break that stereotype! Surprise them! Show students that you are on their side!

11. Be reliable and trustworthy.

Keep your promises. Do what you say you are going to do. Be someone kids can count on. Don't gossip. Fiercely protect confidences. Follow through.

12. Be trusting.

Let students take appropriate responsibilities. Then trust them to be able to carry them out. You can demonstrate trust by finding

> I feel disrespected when the teacher tells the class something I told her in confidence.
> – Susan, grade 8

opportunities to give students significant voice in their classroom operation and in their learning. Chapter 11 discusses student voice and choice in depth and gives many strategies for doing this. You show and build respect when you give students some real power over their lives in the classroom and over their learning. Then trust them to do the tasks they have agreed to take on.

13. Ask for their opinions.

Don't be afraid to ask students what they think about certain situations, even those situations in which they have something to say about you. Once when a student in an after-school program spoke to one of our adults in a disrespectful tone, I told the student that he would have to leave. When he left, I turned to the group and asked them if they thought that I was being fair. It was a great conversation. Some students felt that my action was appropriate; others felt that I had "called him out" in front of his peers, and, therefore, he was going to react. Needless to say, the adults in the room learned plenty from listening to students' opinions. And the students felt that we were respecting their voice and opinions. (A cautionary note: In this kind of a situation, make it clear to students that you are soliciting their input—not asking them to make decisions about how you will handle this particular student.)

14. Help students succeed.

When I ask students to describe what respect from a teacher looks like, many of the responses have to do with the teacher helping students learn. When you show that you believe a student can achieve, he feels respected. When you help a student master something or reach a goal, she feels respected. Students know that it is your job to help them learn. **They respect you when you do your job.** They also feel respect from you—that they were worth your time and trust. And their self-respect is enhanced, too. One of the best things you can do in a classroom is to identify an individual's learning needs and goals, and then help the student meet them.

> I feel respected when the teacher gives full instructions and explains things clearly.
> – Chance, grade 7

If You Can't Manage Them . . .

15. **Start fresh every day.**

Let yesterday's issues belong to yesterday. Let each student start a new day—without fearing that you will hold over judgments, annoyances, grudges, or remembrances of misbehavior from other days. Make sure the consequences are properly enforced, then let

go of the issue or infraction. Each child should feel free to enter your class with renewed hope and a new chance for a good day. Students will feel respected when you do them the honor of expecting that each day will be a good one for them—even if they had a major screw-up yesterday.

Student Self-Respect

Lack of self-respect is at the root of much rude behavior or misbehavior. Persons who do not respect others generally do not respect themselves. Lack of self-respect is a major factor behind bullying. Disrespectful persons of any age—whether or not they are classified as a bully—often try to demand respect. But what they get is not satisfying. And this frustrating inability to get respect can erupt as anger.

There are few tasks as important as helping a child deepen her self-respect. It is a hard thing to "teach" because the roots of a student's self-respect are formed deep in early childhood and through a wide range of important social interactions. But a student with self-respect will have more rewarding social interactions, will more likely contribute to a respectful classroom, and will be better able to reach his or her academic potential.

This class bully needs a dose of self-respect.

In the classroom, you can set processes and create situations to nurture students' self-respect. One of the most basic strategies is to follow the kinds of advice given so far in this chapter for creating a climate of respect. This is the best kind of setting for deepening feelings of self-value.

Here are some specific goals and strategies you can pursue for nourishing self-respect:

- Allow for and encourage independence—in students' work and thinking.
- Give students responsibility; trust them to handle it.
- Set strong expectations for respecting one another, and hold students to them.
- Build individuals' self-confidence by helping them succeed in their studies.
- Do everything you can to help each student experience a sense of belonging.
- Be honest.

If You Can't Manage Them . . .

- Celebrate student accomplishments.
- Identify and affirm personal qualities.
- When you discipline a student, focus on the action, not on the child's character or person.
- Encourage students not to give up. Give assistance so they can succeed.
- Help them set reasonable, attainable goals.
- Affirm choices and decisions that are healthy for the student.
- Ask for student input. Tell them that their opinions matter.
- Tell them that wrong behavior does not make them "bad."
- Listen to students and validate their feelings.

Student-to-Student Respect

Now we come to the really important link on the respect chain—students treating each other with respect! Without plenty of student-to-student respect, your classroom will be an unpleasant place for all the inhabitants. However, by this point in the chain, your students will have had plenty of good lessons about respect. Some teachers feel that the most important thing in classroom management is for students to behave respectfully toward the teacher. I am much more concerned with how they treat each other.

In this section, I will focus on teaching respect, because it is in the context of the students relating to each other that respect is best taught.

1. **Model respect.**

   The first way to teach respect, as I have already shown, is for **the teacher to model it**. Innumerable respect lessons are taught this way.

   Here are some other ways to teach respect among students:

2. **Define respect.**

   Go back to the beginning of this chapter, and share the definitions and descriptions with students. Define *disrespect* as well.

   I feel disrespected when students leave me out.
   – Greta, grade 8

3. **Discuss respect.**

   Talk about respect. Do this the first day of school. Start the conversation about what respect is and how it looks in school. Keep the discussion going all year long. Discuss it in the whole group and in small groups. Talk about what it is. Talk about its opposite—disrespect. Deal with words such as *contempt, disdain, honor, esteem, value,* and *discount.* Talk about how it feels to be the recipient of disrespect.

4. **Make respect personal.**

   Ask students to give examples from their own experiences. You give examples. Ask students to act out examples of respect. Ask them to show how respect feels and how disrespect feels. Ask them to tell how they know when they get respect and when they do not.

If You Can't Manage Them . . .

5. Make respecting one anther a classroom rule.

Make it the most important classroom rule. Talk about respect as a basic right of human beings. Make sure students are clear about the consequences of not following the rule.

> If you do not respond to disrespect, your silence will reinforce it.

6. Expect respect.

Show students early and clearly that respect is expected. But make sure they know what you mean by this. Don't assume they will do it if they don't fully understand it.

7. Notice respect. Respond to it.

Keep your eyes open all the time for demonstrations of respect. Affirm these. State what it is you see that is respectful.

8. Notice disrespect. Respond to it.

Do not allow disrespect—even what may seem like minor incidences—to go unrecognized. Do not tolerate it. Consistently apply the consequences that have been outlined. If you do not respond to disrespect, your silence will reinforce it.

9. Elaborate on respect.

Extend the discussion of respect to more subtle manifestations. Discuss its connection to respect for opinions, beliefs, likes and dislikes, skills and abilities, interests, cultural backgrounds, and racial and gender and sexual identity differences. Encourage students to see how variety makes life more interesting.

Talk about manifestations of disrespect that may seem harmless: laughing at someone behind his or her back, mimicking someone, making fun of someone privately to a friend, talking while someone is talking, teasing someone, pressuring someone to do something that is against his wishes or beliefs— or something she just does not want to do.

10. Talk about the power of words.

Students and others are often oblivious about the power of their words. Bring this to the front of the discussion. Think about what words can do. Find examples of words that can elevate, hurt, embarrass, comfort, encourage, or demean. Students can build a list of words and phrases (appropriate to write or say in school) that they will commit to use or not use.

11. Build an activity around respect.

Don't underestimate either the power or the necessity of specific lessons that examine and promote respect among students. Here are a few suggestions. Once you get started, other ideas will flow. Don't neglect to pull students into the creating of such activities. They'll have great ideas!

• • • • Media Scan

The culture is full of models of disrespect. Use examples from the genres and sources that are a part of students' lives. Find some clips from movies or TV shows. Have students track down ads, apps, YouTube videos, and song lyrics. Look for examples of respect and disrespect.

Share these. Ask questions such as:

- *What is happening here?*
- *Who shows respect? Who shows disrespect?*
- *How do you know?*
- *Where else have you seen similar behavior?*
- *Do you do this? Do your friends do this? Why? What is the impact?*
- *How does this feel for the person being respected (or disrespected)?*
- *What are (or will be) the consequences of the incident or actions you just saw, heard, or read?*
- *Why are people sometimes disrespectful to one another?*

• • • • Recipe for Respect

Let students work in groups or pairs to create a recipe for respect in the classroom. Ask them to think carefully about the ingredients and the behaviors or steps for putting the recipe together. Suggest that they think about how and where to serve it! Encourage them to illustrate the recipe.

• • • • Respect Collage

Get a stack of newspapers and magazines. Students can find words, phrases, titles, and images that communicate respect. This will take some ingenuity! Give them space to display their creations and time to comment on them.

• • • • Disagreement without Disrespect

Each day, I try to present and discuss a current event, especially those current events that are contentious and controversial. I believe it is important to provide opportunities for our students to grapple with issues that their parents and society are discussing. It is also very important that I model and help students learn how to communicate with one another respectfully even when they disagree with one another (a skill many of our national leaders struggle to develop.)

I vividly remember one student who had very strong opinions about every subject and was never afraid to share those opinions even when he stood alone. (I had to admire him for that, especially in a middle school classroom). However, the young man also believed he was always right and literally would make faces and noises (yes, noises) every time someone disagreed with his opinion. What he was doing was disrespectful to his classmates and yet I felt that if I addressed his behavior, I might shut him down entirely. He had every right to his opinion, but he did not have the right to be disrespectful to his peers.

> I feel respected when people engage with me in conversation.
> – Sinal, grade 9

After much reflection and discussion with my colleagues, I decided that I needed to address his behavior privately. Naturally it happened the next day; so I asked him to stay for a minute after class. We had a great conversation and I specifically identified exactly what he was doing. (It is crucial to be precise with students about what the behavior is that you deem as inappropriate.) I ended the conversation by telling him that I loved his willingness to share his

If You Can't Manage Them . . .

opinion, but that it was important for him to demonstrate respect to his peers just as they did to him. Consequences for his disrespectful behavior were spelled out and applied. By the end of the year, he was able to listen to his peers without making faces and noises.

While the class is discussing a current event or particular issue, I do not tolerate yelling, interrupting, or put-downs. There are consequences for those behaviors—which may include, after a warning, stopping the current event discussion for the day or week. Other students do not like this consequence, so at times, I may move the student to the hall until our discussion is complete.

• • • • Different Doesn't Mean Bad

This is an activity I have used to illustrate the need to respect our differences.

1. Gather several colors of markers and several sheets of white computer paper with an empty bar graph printed on the paper. The graph has a wide, empty bar for *Yes* and an empty bar for *No*.

2. Create different statements and write one on each sheet. Tape the sheets around the room (see examples on page 83). Make about half the number of graphs as the number of students you have (e.g., 15 graphs for 30 students). See page 88 for an example.

3. Assign two students to each statement. Explain to students that they will respond to the

statement by using their marker to color a small portion on the empty bar that best represents each of them as individuals. Model this for the class. Give students about 15 seconds at each graph and then call, "Rotate." Explain the direction that the class will rotate.

4. Once all students have addressed the statements and colored the graph, ask the following questions: "What do you see?" "What does this tell you about our class?" (Answers will include such ideas as: that there are many different responses, or that not all students answered in the same way.)

5. Explain to the class that all of us come to this room with different interests and different strengths. We need to respect and accept the differences in each of us.

   Examples of statements:

   I am good at math.

   I like to read.

   I can speak another language.

   I've traveled to another country.

   I can fix things when they break.

   I like to dance.

   I am a good artist.

   I'm good at most sports.

   I am confident when I speak in front of others.

   I like animals.

I am able to listen to the teacher and remember the information.

I like to learn by doing hands-on activities.

I have stepsisters, stepbrothers, or stepparents.

I do my homework the day I get it.

At the beginning of the year, use low-risk statements so students can feel safe and comfortable as they adjust to your classroom. Once you have built a community feeling within the class, you can try some higher-risk statements.

• • • • Happiness Sheets

I use this activity near the end of the year as a way to incorporate positive affirmations among the students in my class. But you can use it any time after the students have had a chance to get to know each other.

1. Give each student a sheet of paper. At the top of the paper they will write their first and last names in somewhat bigger letters than they would normally use.

2. Explain the rotation system you expect them to use. Make sure you as the teacher are also involved.

3. Talk about what positive affirmations are and give several examples of the kinds they may want to write on their classmates' papers. An example I give is that it is more powerful to write "I like your smile" than it is to write "I like you."

4. When you tell them to begin, the students will pass papers to the person in front of them. That student will write a positive affirmation about the person whose name is at the top.

5. Students MUST sign their names after each affirmation. (This eliminates negative comments.)

6. I usually give about 20 seconds before I call for a rotation.

7. Once every student has had a chance to respond to his or her peers, give them time to read the affirmations from their peers.

• • • • **Respect on Display**

After you have talked about respect for a while, ask students to compile posters that answer this question: "What does respect look like in the classroom?" Students can work in small groups, and if you wish, you can consolidate the ideas into one large poster. They can specify components of classroom respect, or combine them. For example, a poster could be titled "What does respect look like from teacher to student?" (or, from student to teacher, or from student to student).

They can also create posters answering the question, "What does disrespect look like?" or "What do teachers do that is disrespectful?" or "What do students do that is disrespectful?" On the next two pages, see examples of posters based on ideas from my students.

What Does Respect Look Like?

Student to Teacher

- Student accepts responsibility for his or her part in a situation.
- Student follows the procedures, routines, and rules of the classroom.
- Student participates in the activities presented by the teacher.
- Student is open to constructive suggestions from the teacher.
- Student addresses the teacher by name.
- Student takes turns talking in class.
- Student says *hello* to teacher.
- Student says *please* and *thank you.*
- Student comes to class on time.
- Student comes to class prepared.

Teacher to Student

- Teacher actively listens without interrupting the student.
- Teacher listens to the student's side of the issue.
- Teacher greets each student and pronounces each name correctly.
- Teacher recognizes that fair is not always equal.
- Teacher remembers and inquires about what's going on in students' personal lives.
- Teacher never calls parents without first informing the student.
- Teacher gives students chances to solve their own problems and does not underestimate them.
- Teacher talks to students in private about problems.
- Teacher earns respect by being fair and consistent.

Student to Student

- Student actively listens to input and feedback from classmates.
- Student participates without interrupting other students.
- Student offers to help classmates rather than just give them answers.
- Student encourages classmates.
- Student comments appropriately on what other students say during discussions.
- Student accepts all other students.
- Student sticks up for other students.
- Student does not call others names.
- Students notice each other as valuable persons.
- Student honors other students' differences.

What Teachers Do
That Is Disrespectful

- Punish the entire group for the actions of a few.
- Mock students as a method of discipline.
- Use embarrassment as a disciplinary tool.
- Use sarcasm as a put-down.
- Discipline one student in front of all the others.
- Show favoritism.
- Don't believe a student can do something.
- Talk to students like they are infants.
- Put on a "teacher" mask or use a "teacher" voice.
- Talk about students behind their backs.

What Kids Do
That Is Disrespectful

- Speak in a rude tone.
- Roll eyes when being talked to.
- Refuse to do what the teacher has asked them to do.
- Interrupt or blurt out during class lessons.
- Harass or make fun of other students.
- Swear.
- Ignore other students.
- Talk back to the teacher.

If You Can't Manage Them . . .

Example

Different Doesn't Mean BAD!

*When I take a test, I feel confident
when there are essay questions on the test.*

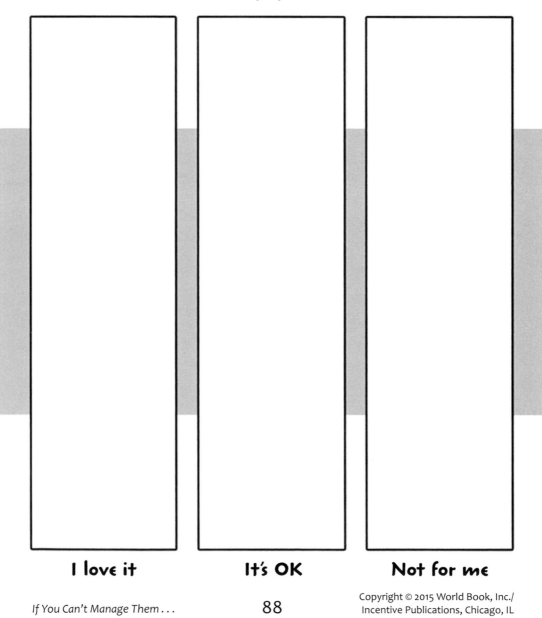

I love it   **It's OK**   **Not for me**

Student-to-Teacher Respect

So here we are at the component of classroom respect that seems most important to some teachers. My belief (as you have certainly picked up by now) is that **all** relationships within the classroom are equally important. The teacher deserves the same level of respect as every other person in the classroom—but not necessarily any more.

By the time we get to this point on the respect chain (which is actually a respect circle), student-to-teacher respect is not difficult to address or put into practice. Students should be respectful to adults—not because they are adults—but because they are human beings deserving of respect.

> The teacher deserves the same level of respect as every other person in the classroom.

In your classroom, you can expect students to respect you because you have really worked at creating a climate of mutual respect with techniques such as those discussed in this chapter. But what about adults who have not demonstrated this kind of respect toward students? Make sure students understand that it is right to meet disrespect with respect—that they are to treat adults respectfully, even if they do not like them.

In the real school world, where adults are the authority figures, students need to be especially aware of the necessity to treat adults with respect—or they will surely have troubles. Dedicate some discussions and lessons just to the topic of student-to-adult respect. Make sure students understand that this relates to all adults in the school.

If You Can't Manage Them . . .

Students need clear examples of student-to-teacher respect, just as they need to see what respect from teacher-to-student and student-to-student looks like. I do this by setting up scenarios involving respectful or disrespectful behavior (or by inviting a student to help by acting out a scenario).

Example: *I ask a student, for the second time, to take her seat. The student rolls her eyes and huffs as she moves toward her seat.*

I ask the class: "Would this be considered disrespectful? Why or why not?"

Then I explain what a reaction like this tells me: "Her nonverbal signals and her body language say that she is disgusted with me, doesn't like me at this moment, and doesn't want to do what I just asked her to do." Students need to understand that disrespect can be demonstrated with nonverbal responses just as clearly as with rude words.

Example: *I encourage a student to get started on his work. He responds in a very sarcastic tone (I demonstrate the tone), "Yea, yea. I will in a minute."*

Again I ask the students: "Would this be considered disrespectful? Why or why not?"

I explain: "His tone of voice tells me that he does not like what I just said, does not think of me as the leader in the classroom, or does not think that I have the right to tell him what to do in the classroom." Then I remind students that it is not always **what** you say that can be disrespectful; **how** you say it can also show disrespect.

Example: *During a class discussion, a student is incessantly talking to his neighbor. I ask him please to stop talking. He responds sarcastically, "What? I wasn't talking."*

Once more I ask the students: "Would this be considered disrespectful? Why or why not?"

I explain: "This response tells me that the student thinks that I am not telling the truth, or that I did not clearly see what was happening." I tell my students that this is a way of insulting me, and demanding that I give in to what I know is wrong, or start an argument with the student. This argumentative denial is disrespectful.

What, then, does respectful behavior look like? Students need demonstrations of this to accompany the examples of disrespect. "I'm sorry, Ms. Campbell, . . ." will earn them much more respect from me than an argument. An apology also merits a very quick return to normal feelings between the student and teacher. However, I also tell them that an apology means nothing if the behavior does not change.

Many times a day, I remind students that honesty is respect. I tell them that I will be honest with them and that they need to be honest with me. I promise to admit when I am wrong, and I tell them that I expect the same from them. I stress to them that as they learn to admit when they are wrong, take responsibility, and accept the consequences, they show respect to their peers and me, and in turn earn respect from us. Acceptance is part of maturing and part of the way our classroom needs to operate.

If You Can't Manage Them . . .

This respect extends to all adults in the classroom and school. I make sure my students hear this frequently. Many classrooms have paraprofessionals. I introduce the paraprofessional and tell students that this person is an important member of our classroom community. I make a point to students that if any adult in the school asks for cooperation, I expect that each student will comply respectfully.

I feel respected when a student introduces his or her parents to me.

Kim,
middle school teacher

In his book *The 55 Essentials*, Ron Clark suggests that students learn the names of all the adults in the school (2003). This includes teachers, secretaries, kitchen staff, paraprofessionals, administrators, volunteers, and maintenance staff. Personally introduce the adults in your building to your students. This demonstrates to students your respect for these adults and affirms their importance as members of the school community.

Periodically, I will introduce two or three staff members and explain what they do in our building. I challenge the students to create shock and awe with the adults in the building by using their names and giving a quick "hello" when they see them in the hallways or in their workplaces.

Look and behave like an adult. It is hard for students to respect you as an adult or perceive you as an authority figure if you do not behave as an adult. Be an adult. Talk like an adult. Dress like an adult.

A few years ago a young, right-out-of-college female was hired as our high school social studies teacher. She was petite, blond, hip, and fun, and looked 16 at the very most. Immediately she began to have discipline issues, and my phone began to ring, both from her and her principal. After spending some time observing her in the classroom, it became obvious that she was experiencing some typical new-teacher problems, such as lack of follow-through, inconsistent messages, lack of clear instructions, and so on. However, I also noticed how she was dressed—low-riding jeans, a tight T-shirt, and flip-flops. (Oh, the joys of being young!) Seriously, I knew her choice of attire was going to be a part of our discussion.

During our post-observation discussion, she told me (with a smile on her face) that she continually gets stopped by the high school hall monitors asking her where she's supposed to be and requesting to see her hall pass. It's not until she shows them her ID that they believe her, she told me. This was the opening I needed.

I began by explaining to her that it was possible that some of her management issues were presenting themselves because she looked young, fit, fun, and more like a student than a teacher (all characteristics we veteran teachers envy). I explained the predicament: Looking so young was putting her at a disadvantage because students were seeing her as one of them instead of the authority in the classroom. I recommended that she take immediate steps to look more mature. This happens a lot with young teachers. They are prejudged as lacking experience, and, hey, it's probably true, right? Changing the manner of dress to look more professional benefits the teacher and makes lines clearer to the students. It also helps to gain respect from colleagues and parents. (Parents hope you appear wise, tasteful, adult, and responsible in front of their impressionable teenagers.)

This issue is not unique to new or young teachers. I see many veteran teachers who come to school every day in jeans, sweatshirts, and clothes that one would wear at home in the garden. This seems to be a poor way to represent the teaching profession— which is clearly under attack on many fronts. We should do everything we can to exemplify professionalism, confidence, and integrity.

The way a teacher dresses is a subtle and easy way to exert influence in the classroom. If the attire is

Mr. A might have trouble earning respect from his students today.

overly casual or sloppy, he shows low esteem for himself, his students, and his profession. Students may assume they can treat a casually dressed teacher in a casual manner, or that classroom rules can be casually followed. I am old-fashioned enough to believe that a teacher who dresses for success will communicate that it is an honor to be an educator. Avoid clothing that is too short or tight, flip-flops, tank tops, and any clothing that shows your midriff when you raise your arms or reveals cleavage when you bend over. Don't dress like the kids, even if that is how you dress when you go out on the town.

When you ask students to respect all adults, make sure they see you doing the same. Students are watching your responses to parents and colleagues. (They may also overhear your cell phone calls and your conversations with other adults.) They will notice disapproval, disrespect, disgust, annoyance, gossip, sarcasm, facial expressions, body language, and tone of voice. While you are giving them speeches about respecting all adults in the school, be sure you are showing respect for all school staff members (and parents and visitors) with your language, actions, and attitude. Follow the rules of the school. Do not gossip. Show esteem for colleagues. Treat parents kindly. Respect your authority figures.

If You Can't Manage Them . . .

Unfortunately, in our culture, the idea of respect has changed—or, in some cases, the emphasis on it. My students tell me that to be respected, a teacher must earn respect. Yes, that is true . . . so make sure you do earn it. But we also must constantly repeat the message that all persons deserve respect, even if they are not working hard to earn it.

> I feel respected when I am noticed as existing.
> – Lily, grade 8

Plan to include the topic of respect early, regularly, and all year long in your classroom. Go back to page 58 and review the strategies you listed. If they are working, be sure to strengthen them and keep using them. Expand your repertoire with more ideas from this chapter. Such efforts will be gifts you give to your students and to yourself. Contempt (the opposite of respect) is powerful and destructive. Drive it out with relentless respect. You will have taken a huge step toward successful classroom management.

Chapter 4

Preparation

The bell rings—and you're ON!

Am I Ready?

Take the survey. Answer the questions honestly.

Absolutely Sometimes Rarely

1. When I need to find something on my desk, I can find it quickly.

2. At all times, I keep a good supply of general materials students may need (such as glue, pencils, tape, pencil sharpeners, tissues).

3. When I start a class, I have a carefully prepared agenda for the entire class.

4. If I need copies for my next day's lesson, I make them the day before.

5. I gather all materials for the day's classes or lessons well ahead of time.

6. When I plan a unit of study, I map out an outline of the unit (including assessments).

7. I think through and note steps for each of my lessons.

8. The night before, I make a list of things to do during my prep period.

9. Before I start a lesson, I am ready for possible glitches, individual differences, and alterations that may arise.

10. I have five or more minutes to focus mentally before the first bell in the morning.

The recurring nightmare:

After being stuck in traffic because of a long accident-related detour, I arrive at school just 15 minutes before the first bell. I race to the copy machine with my folder of study guides and worksheets for the day's classes. Somehow I just can't hurry. My feet feel glued to the floor. Too many people try to stop me to chat. The copy machine jams. I unclog it. It jams again. I race to the next building. This machine is out of paper. Dodging incoming students, I race back toward my room. No wonder I'm moving slowly—I'm still wearing slippers. I catch my reflection in the glass on the door. I'm still in my pajamas. A parent with a worried look on her face is waiting at my door. Students are streaming in. I've left all the materials for my lesson in my car. The bell rings. I'm frozen. Students are laughing and throwing things. The parent stands in the doorway—staring. The bell keeps ringing.

> The person who moves mountains begins by carrying small stones.
>
> – Ancient Chinese Proverb

This nightmare is not limited to inexperienced teachers. It is not even limited to the world of dreams. Unfortunately, many teachers live this nightmare. I've lived it too many times myself! Class gets off to a terrible start, and it's all my doing. Not one of the problems is precipitated by unruly or uncooperative students. But if I am at all interested in the welfare of students (or, for that matter, in self-survival), I have to stop repeating the nightmare in my waking hours. And then I might find that it fades from my dreams as well.

This is a critical piece of classroom management: The teacher must be prepared and organized for each day, each class, each lesson—all the way through. Students (particularly adolescents) will sense the lack of preparation and capitalize on it immediately. If you are not ready, chaos is guaranteed.

If You Can't Manage Them . . .

Do Everyone a Favor

Plan to be fully ready when that bell rings. You'll do students a whole lot of favors, and you'll reap plenty of benefits yourself. Here are some of the things that happen when you are organized and ready for each day and each class:

- You demonstrate to students that you are ready for them.
- They can feel that you want them to be there.
- Students enter a place of calm (though lively) security—not chaotic frenzy.
- You are free to be at the door, available for relating to students—a welcoming way for their class to begin.
- Learning begins as soon as students arrive. This shows students that you take their learning seriously and that this is what you are here to do.
- Your readiness shows enthusiasm about the work of the day. Students get the idea that you are energized and ready to go— not scattered and reluctant to be there!
- Students get the idea that you are the leader. This provides safety for students, and sets a tone for good management.
- You model organization and promptness—something students need to learn and internalize.
- Students experience consistency—something they need in a chaotic world—something that helps them be calm, secure, and ready to learn.
- You do a better job of teaching, because you are focused and unstressed.
- You avoid a whole lot of potential delays, disruptions, and problems that will occur if there is uncertainty or confusion about class getting underway.

At the Beginning . . .

Before the school year begins, and as you are getting ready for students to arrive, plan an environment that is

- safe—emotionally and physically
- conducive to learning—orderly, calm, stimulating
- likely to reduce, rather than increase, problems

- **Think ahead about the daily activities** and events in the classroom. Make a list of these— such things as entering, leaving, getting materials, collecting papers, returning papers to students, accounting for homework, taking attendance, disposing of trash, sharpening pencils, or using supplies. Plan for ways to make each of these events run efficiently and smoothly.

- **Anticipate distractions or interruptions.** Make a list of these—such things as student need for hall passes, knocks on the door, people dropping by to drop something off, messages that need to be sent to the office, someone getting sick, new student appearing at the door in the middle of a lesson, power failures, or technological device that stops working. Don't wait until one of these happens to figure out how you will respond. Have a plan in place. (Of course, you can't prepare for every possible event. You can, however, anticipate most of them—if you have been through all or part of one school year as a teacher.)

If You Can't Manage Them . . .

> If you are organized and prepared, learning begins as soon as students enter your room.

- **Write up a supply list.** Note and gather the general supplies that you will need to have available for students through the year. This might include items such as paper, pencils, math tools, tissues, markers, folders, and such. Keep this list handy so you can note when things get low and need resupply. Create a system for resupplying so that you don't get into a lesson that needs drawing supplies with no drawing paper, or you don't get into flu season without tissues.

- **Arrange the room for minimizing problems.** In one of my most memorable teacher-preparation classes, the professor proclaimed something that I remember as this: "Your classroom arrangement can cause more management issues than your worst-behaved students." She was right! The placement of student seats, location of the teacher's desk, width of space between furniture, where things face, location of supplies, placement of information on walls—all can be the root of many conflicts or disruptions. And all of the physical arrangement components interact with many other things such as the lengths of arms and legs, body size and body odor, friendships, rivalries, and fears.

So when you set up your room, give thought to:

- the width of aisles between desks
- space for outstretched legs

- traffic patterns to the door, to the supply area, to the pencil sharpener
- student line of vision to all presentations
- teacher visual access to all students
- unobstructed access to supplies and information
- student access to the teacher
- the need for private teacher–student conversations

Consider these practices:

1. Allow as much space between rows and groups of desks as you possibly can.

2. Actually draw a flowchart of traffic patterns to see how they will work.

3. Make sure that you can see all students from your desk or any other place you might linger to talk with individuals.

4. Make sure every student can see you, the board or screen, the active board, or any other presentation spot.

5. Keep an extra desk somewhat near your desk or near the area you tend to spend more time. You can use this for a visitor, or for a student who needs some "time away" from her or his regular seating.

6. Create a bit of private space near your desk. Have a chair where a student can sit with back to the group, facing you—for private chats about his or her work.

7. Place supplies in one general area so students do not have to wander around the room to get things.

If You Can't Manage Them . . .

8. Post notices, reminders, and critical information near the door so students see it as they leave.

9. Place a container of some sort outside your door or on your door for nonconfidential memos, reminders, or other papers to be left. That way, every visitor will not have to actually enter your room.

MR. GORDON, CLASS STARTED 15 MINUTES AGO!

HUH?

10. As you get to know students, develop a repertoire of arrangements for seats and specific seating assignments for students. You will learn what configurations work for minimizing distractions. You will learn what pairings or groupings of students do or do not work well for good learning.

Weeks Ahead of a Unit . . .

Long before you kick off a unit of study or a series of lessons—get organized. Most teachers are used to planning the concepts and activities that will be part of a unit. But often, teachers are not thinking of this process as a matter of good learning PLUS good management.

- • • • **Collaborate with colleagues.** Discuss upcoming units of studies with others in your department. Coordinate plans with other members of your interdisciplinary team. Your students do go to other teachers. It's best for the students if these other teachers know what your kids will be studying. Beyond that, colleagues can find ways to reinforce what students are learning and connect concepts from other disciplines where possible.

Furthermore, you can think through the logistics of a unit with teammates or colleagues. This can help avoid distractions and glitches before they happen.

- **Start any unit plan by defining goals.** Exactly what is it that each student will gain from the unit as a whole and each activity in it? My colleagues and I use a strategy called "the essential question." We ask ourselves, "What question do we want our students to be able to answer at the end of the unit?" Every lesson we create throughout the unit should in some way attempt to answer the essential question. (You can use this approach for any individual lesson as well as for unit planning.)

If you want to manage a middle school classroom, you have to be really organized.
– Shelby, grade 9

Here are a few samples of questions we have posed as the goal of a unit:

- *How does colonialism affect a country and its people?*
- *What are four reasons why some countries struggle to develop?*
- *How could both the Israelis' claim and the Palestinians' claim to land in Israel be justified?*

My current principal, Dr. Shirley Gregoire, has another suggestion for establishing goals. She noticed that when she asked teachers to describe goals of a unit or lesson, they tended to start explaining their lessons. Instead of defining goals, they described activities. So she asks this instead: "When your students walk into your classroom, each student has a set of skills and knowledge. When they leave your classroom, how has their knowledge or skill changed?" That answer, she says, is the goal of the lesson.

- **Make a list of activities and strategies** that you will use to meet your established goals and objectives. Make sure that each one helps to answer the essential question!

- **Determine the logical order of the activities** to meet your goals. Sketch out this order, ON PAPER, so you can be prepared throughout the week. This doesn't mean things won't change, but at least it gives you a road map to follow.

- **Create a unit calendar.** Be sure to mark early or late starts, vacations, assemblies, and other such interruptions to the normal schedule. On the calendar, note what you will do each day that relates to the essential question of the unit. It is best to create this calendar on a computer so that you can make changes easily. Lesson lengths, activities, new ideas, field trip plans, guest speakers' schedules, school schedule alterations, and such create almost a daily need to update the calendar.

- **Start a supply list.** As you create the calendar, keep track of everything you will need for each learning activity. (Your list might include things such as: Schedule field trip to the planetarium. Reserve computer time. Get building supplies for geometric models. Make copies of study guides. Order DVDs.)

- **Reserve supplies.** Once you have established your calendar, track down and reserve materials you will need for each lesson. Veteran teachers will tell you that if you plan to use the computer lab in January, you'd better reserve your dates the previous September.

- **Schedule and prepare other details.** Start planning and making digital presentations. Schedule field trips. Arrange for chaperones. Purchase any supplies needed or send out requests for donations. Get permission slips ready for field trips. Prepare study guides, unit outlines, independent study options, assessments, project guidelines, and other materials students will use. With each piece you prepare, keep asking the question: "Will this activity or event help students move toward an answer to the essential question?"

My best classroom management advice for the teacher? Have everything prepared before the kids arrive!
– Tierra, grade 8

If your school has a study hall, don't be afraid to borrow services of study hall students who are doing okay in their classes. (They can do many different tasks for you—cut out shapes, put up a new bulletin board, research dates, collate papers, prepare folders of materials, make samples, put digital presentations together for you, and so on.) Ask the study hall teacher which students are the most responsible and bring them on board. The helping students will love this!

If You Can't Manage Them . . .

- **Identify the vocabulary words** that students will need to understand the material in the upcoming unit or lesson. You can start on this list as soon as you have established the essential question(s) for your unit. The more background knowledge you provide, such as understanding of terminology, the easier it will be for students to comprehend the concepts in the unit.

A Day or Two Ahead . . .

A unit, lesson, or series of lessons can sneak up on you. Never leave your planning until the day of the lesson. To keep on your trajectory of smooth lessons and minimal management problems, take care of these last-minute things BEFORE the last minute.

THE TESTS YOU TOOK LAST MONTH?

I'M SURE I HANDED THOSE BACK!

- **Resupply and recheck.** Check your list of general supplies for the room. You may have done a meticulous job of gathering materials for the unit. But you will still have slowdowns and disruptions if you have not kept up with the regular supplies of the classroom. Check all technological devices and programs that you need for upcoming lessons. Open the container to be sure that the software program really is inside! Run it to see that it is working! Don't wait until you get into the presentation to figure out that you needed a backup bulb or a screen that's not broken or pens for the active board.

- **Return all necessary papers.** This is crucial at the beginning of the unit, and for any lesson within a unit or any other type of lesson or activity. See that you have graded and returned any work students have done that involves background knowledge or preparation for this particular lesson or unit. In fact, make it a policy to have all work back to students within two days of collecting it from them.

- **Make the best use of your prep period.** Each evening, make a list of tasks that need to be done the next day during your prep period. The list will avoid wasted time. For me, this practice keeps me sane! When I leave my classroom, I take my list with me. This is not because I may forget why I went to my office in the first place (yes, that does happen), but rather because as I run into people, I suddenly have a new task added to my list. If I don't add the new task to my list, I will probably forget it by the time I return to my classroom or desk. (By the way, you should know this **will** get worse as you age.)

- **Get copies made at least a day ahead.** Early in my teaching career, I arrived at school one day with a variety of worksheets to duplicate for my first period class. I was shocked to find that the machine was "down"— out of order—kaput—not cooperative! What!!?? Don't they close schools when copy machines are not functioning? I found another machine, got the copies finished just as the bell rang, and raced to my classroom—only to realize that I had left the other pieces of my fantastic lesson on my desk back at my office. Needless to say, I was *not* prepared. And not surprisingly, my middle school students, with their innate ability to sense a weakness, capitalized on it immediately. The bell had barely rung, and chaos already reigned. It was precipitated—not by troublesome students, but by my lack of preparation.

Make copies the night before (or the day before that)—even if you have to stay late. The law of averages (especially where school copy machines are involved) will guarantee that some days there will be a line of teachers at the machine, or the machine will be on holiday. If you are not able to make copies the night before, have a backup plan for your lesson.

- **Anticipate glitches.** Think through the lessons coming up in the next few days. What might happen that will require alterations? Prepare for differences in learning styles. Have alternative activities on hand. Certainly you cannot anticipate every complication that may arise—but many of them you can! You know your students and their needs, fears, hesitations, and gifts. Consider what surprises may occur!

Daily, In Class . . .

Ahh! Everything is ready and in place for great lessons. Oops! That is still not quite enough. All your best plans can result in lessons that fizzle if the organization does not continue into each day's classes. Here are some "must-do's" to get those lessons off to the best start.

- **Start class on time.** Start your class on time. We expect our students to be on time; therefore, it is our absolute responsibility ALWAYS to start on time. This is WAY important! This simple practice establishes you as the person in charge. It tells students that the academic tasks of the day are important. It sends the message to students that they come to class to learn. It shows students that you are organized and ready to go (a good habit for students to watch in practice). It leaves no time for troubles to brew.

I have a colleague who struggles with starting class on time and, because of this, various discipline issues arise each day. When we were discussing this one afternoon, I asked, "What keeps you from starting your class on time?"

Her answer had nothing to do with a lack of organization. Instead she felt that the start of class was a good time for students to ask her what they had missed when they were absent, clarify their homework, or answer other questions. I shared my observation that students bring tremendous energy into the classroom from their time in the hall—and that the teacher has about one minute to rechannel that energy before it splinters into chaos. Once this opportunity is lost, the teacher will spend a whole lot more time getting the class back in hand—and all that energy that could have gone into learning will be wasted.

> Students bring tremendous energy into the classroom from their time in the hall. The teacher has about one minute to re-channel that energy before it splinters into chaos.

We talked about this, and now this colleague answers questions during a 3-minute break halfway through the class period. To her delight, she has noticed a decrease in behavioral problems at the beginning of class.

As soon as the bell rings, stand in front of your class facing the students, directing them into their seats. When the bell rings in my class, I am saying things such as: "Mary, I need you in your seat." "John, let's go." "I'm ready to start." Simply directing the unprepared and distracted students says to the class: "This class is important, and I have high expectations."

Ninety-five percent of discipline problems occur during the first and last five minutes of class, and more than likely come from five percent of the students (Kunjufu, 2002). Get those five percent properly directed, and reduce the percentage of problems in the first five minutes by being focused and ready to go when the bell rings.

- **Get into the lesson promptly.** Don't let your opening events drag along so as to lose momentum. Take care of necessary housekeeping, check in with students, or do whatever routines you have set with expedience! Grab that adolescent energy fast—and get started learning!

- **SHOW. Don't tell.** Recently, I planned for students to cut their vocabulary words apart for a review activity. I learned quickly that as I was describing what to do, the class was descending into mayhem. Fortunately, I remembered my own advice in a hurry, and had them sit on their hands so I could demonstrate. Once all eyes were on me, I literally showed students what to do. Remember this whenever you have specific DOING expectations of your students. It eliminates the barrage of questions from students who are confused.

You definitely do not want that, because as soon as "Ms. C, what do I do?" begins to reverberate throughout the room, you have created a management issue that could have easily been avoided.

- ● ● ● **Tomorrow is another day.**
  Straighten up your stuff as best you can before leaving your classroom. If your classroom is cluttered and your materials are left scattered, you will use up valuable time tomorrow getting things together. This delays good learning and opens the door for management problems.

TOMORROW I WILL GET ORGANIZED.

Preparation and organization are major partners with classroom management. These are two more of the strong fundamentals to success. We teachers are so busy making big decisions every hour of each school day that we cannot afford to be pulling our lessons and ourselves together at the last minute! The "Keeping Me Sane" organizational tool on page 114 is one I use constantly. It does help to keep me sane! Try this. Try the other strategies in this chapter. When you have had time to implement some of the ideas, retake the "Am I Ready?" survey on page 98 of this chapter. See what has changed!

If You Can't Manage Them . . .

Keeping Me Sane!

Day/Date:

	Class	Papers to Copy	Tech Needs	People to Contact	Evening Tasks
Monday					
Tuesday					
Wednesday					
Thursday					
Friday					
Weekend					

They're not just for cheerleaders.

GIVE ME A *G-E-O-M . . .*

Geometry 1
Period 5

MS. C HAS NEVER QUITE LEFT
HER JR. HIGH CHEERLEADING DAYS BEHIND.

✔ It's Just Automatic!

√ Personal Routines

The alarm rings. Your workday starts. What things are part of your morning routine?

The alarm does not ring. It's a weekend or holiday. What things are part of your routine for those days?

Why do you have these routines?

√ Classroom Routines

List four routines you have established in your classroom. For each one, briefly tell why.

1.

2.

3.

4.

What? What did you say? What?

Where are we going?

How far is it?

Why are we doing this?

Who's going with us?

But what about our sharing time?

Will we have to sit in different spots?

But what about all our stuff?

When will we come back?

What about tomorrow?

Is anyone else going to be there?

How come we can't just stay here?

But what if we don't want to go?

Are you going with us?

This is dumb!

But . . . Ms. C . . . . !!

This is how one of my recent class periods began. And what was the occasion for all this protest and anxiety? I had merely announced that we were going to go to another room for our class that day. You would think I had canceled class, decided to speak in Greek, described a new harsh dress code, told them I was quitting my job, taken away their lunch period for a month, or asked them all to recite the *Declaration of Independence* backward. There was so much angst that I almost ditched my plan for the cool activity I had set up in the other room.

It dawned on me then that I was doing something very threatening—I was changing their routine. The students became insecure with this one change.

(Of course, working with preadolescents and adolescents is rarely "routine." Every day is a new day. Each class has its own personality and needs. Every student brings those lovely hormones that wreak havoc on their moods and the teacher's sanity.) Nevertheless, a break in what routines we have does cause a stir. I have learned to anticipate this!

I was doing something very threatening— I was changing their routine.

What Good Are Routines?

Let's start by getting clear about what a routine is. I'll be discussing procedures, rules, expectations, and consequences in later chapters. Don't confuse any of these with routines. A routine has no right or wrong component to it. It is not about respectful behavior or academic responsibility—even though a routine can further both. Routines are more about a sequence of activities—a schedule or rhythm for doing things. A routine is simply a set of steps for helping something run smoothly—a plan for getting something done.

Let's face it, students do not always come to school ready to sit down and learn (especially middle school and high school students). This does not mean that they don't want to learn. It means that there are lots of other things going on when students arrive in a classroom—if they even can get IN the door in time for class. They want to talk to each other, talk to you, catch up, finish conversations and arguments, avoid work, sleep, nurse their hurts from conflicts in the hallway or at home, and attend to many other social and emotional tasks. This all could easily go on for an entire class period.

Classroom routines provide focus, stress relief, calm, and safety for your students. They help you get to the purpose of the class—which is, of course, to help them learn. Without routines, a lot of learning time can be lost, and many management problems brew right away.

Routines . . .

HAVE YOU HEARD THE ONE ABOUT THE TEACHER AND THE DINOSAUR. . . ?

- reduce your stress, because students know what to do and how to do it without having to wait for you to direct them.

- reduce stress for students, because they know what to do as soon as they enter the room.

- tell students that you are organized and ready to go.

- provide consistency— which all students need.

- get students right into a process that sets a tone and mood for learning.

MR. GREEN'S ROUTINES ARE ALWAYS THE SAME!

- smooth the transition from the hall to the lesson.

If You Can't Manage Them . . .

- give students mental calm to turn their focus to their studies.
- set the stage to channel their energy toward the scintillating learning activities you have planned.
- provide kids the safety of knowing you are in control of the environment.
- help you stay organized.
- cut out a gazillion questions.
- cut out wasted time.

And all of the above benefits will help to avoid or minimize management issues.

Rules of Thumb

Set routines for students, starting the first day of the school year. Let them know clearly the "what" and "why" of the processes. Keep these four guidelines in mind as you develop and implement routines.

One   *Keep routines simple.*

Any routine you put into place should be clear, straightforward, and easy for students to understand. A substitute teacher should be able to come into your room, understand, and follow the routines readily. A new student should be able to pick up the routines the first day and take very few days to get them down. They should be simple enough for students to explain them easily.

Two   *Reduce your work.*

Any routine you create should make less work for you. In her book *Never Work Harder Than Your Students*, Robyn Jackson keeps a downright serious focus on helping students achieve, while encouraging teachers to find ways to ease their own workload (2009). I love to keep this catchy title in mind. So many of us teachers develop routines that add a ton of work for us—training students, keeping records, fussing with details. When you establish a routine, ask yourself, "Will this reduce my workload or increase it?" "Exactly what will I have to do to keep this routine going?" If the answer to either of these is complicated—find a different routine.

Three   *Be flexible.*

You may come up with a routine that seems brilliant— great organization for you and the class, the promise of security and focus for students, and a super path to efficiency and good learning. But if it does not work for you or for your students—get rid of it. Try again. Don't be afraid to try different approaches. Don't be so rigid that you can't let go of something that gets harder and harder to make work. Don't cling to a routine for this class because it worked with last year's group. You very likely may need different routines for different classes this year! A word of caution however: Don't make too many changes in routines too quickly. You don't want to confuse students with many changes. Perhaps wait until the end of a quarter (unless the consequences have become so dreadful that you cannot wait).

If You Can't Manage Them . . .

Four   *Limit the routines.*

For some teachers who love order and structure, it will be tempting to make a routine for everything. Don't get carried away with the neatness of routines. You certainly do not want to have a classroom where the value of a few smooth routines turns into drudgery of sameness. Set routines that are needed for safety, wise time use, and better learning. But take care not to program everything into a repetitive, lifeless regimen.

Our Favorite Routines

I'll share several routines that my students and I have tried and liked. These have helped us feel organized and comfortable. There is nothing sacred, however, about the routines I suggest. Don't confine yourself to these, or even incorporate them at all unless they work for you and your students. Please note that these routines are not necessarily completed at the beginning of the class. If you spend too much time doing the routine stuff right off the bat when class starts, you will lose momentum for a lively learning session!

- **Make a connection.**

    A part of every class routine is the human connection. We take time to greet each other and get a welcome from the teacher. For me, no class can start without a few moments for this. I can never dive straight into taking attendance, looking at an agenda, or starting a warm-up task. The connections between persons must come first. No other routine comes close to this in importance.

● ● ● **Post an agenda every day.**

As students enter the room, an agenda outlining what we will be doing that day is visible for all students to see. This identifies what they will know or be able to do at the end of the class that they did not know or were not able to do when they entered.

For example, students might see that they will learn how to convert fractions to decimals, or that they will broaden their understandings of why people immigrate to new places. The agenda defines learning goals and/or the essential question for the unit. Assigned homework is also specified.

> The persons-to-persons connections must come first. No other routine comes close to this in importance.

On most days, most students enter my room, stop and look at the agenda, and then proceed to their seats. My students like to know what is expected of them on any given day. A fringe benefit is that the agenda keeps me focused on the plan for the day. When I first started teaching, I was always rummaging through my plan book to figure out what was coming next. Now it's right in front of my eyes!

- **Start with a question of the day.**

  These days, I get my students pulled into focusing their brains (and settling into the idea that class has started) by asking a question of the day. Today my question was, "If you could meet any world leader, who would it be? Or would it be the president of your country?"

  We take a couple of minutes for everyone to give an answer. Then I move to the front of the room and get on to reviewing the agenda.

- **Review the agenda together.**

  Draw students' attention to the agenda. "Walk" through it quickly. This only takes a minute—a minute well spent by explaining your plans for the day. This is a great time for you to show your enthusiasm for the upcoming events of the class!

- **Get that homework assignment down!**

  If your school uses some sort of planner for students to keep track of their assignments, make sure students get the assignment written in the planner. (If you don't use planners, establish some consistent place for homework assignments.) My students do this during the first discussion about the agenda. I find that waiting until the end of the period doesn't work too well. Students are less focused. Often time runs out, and you even forget to remind them.

Be deliberate about this. Specifically direct student attention to this and make sure they all do it. I realize that it seems like a "no-brainer" to clearly communicate the homework assignment. But many teachers leave this until the end of class, then realize they have run out of time and frantically try to explain to students while the students are busy cleaning up, packing up, and making a dash to line up at the door. It's not that when parents ask their kids after school what homework they have, the students have no clue. This isn't all the fault of the students. Some of the responsibility lies in our hands if we don't find the right moment to adequately assign and articulate the homework assignment.

Let surprise snatch you and students away from routine when the moment calls for it.

● ● ● ● **Cherish the folder.**

In my class, every student has a folder that never leaves the room. I ask them to bring two folders to class the first week of school. I have several on hand for students who don't have them, can't afford them, or forget to bring them. The folder holds notes taken in class, handouts, and other materials that students do not need to take home. When it is time for a test or quiz, they find the related

If You Can't Manage Them . . .

papers in their folders and take them home for review. The folder stays.

Students write the grading scale, classroom expectations, and some of my favorite quotes on the inside or outside of their folders. This cuts out the need for me to give them more papers with these things. It also keeps these important items in front of their eyes every day.

Each day, I place a "Pass Out Folders" sign on two rows of desks. This means that the students sitting in those rows are responsible for handing out the folders before the bell rings. The next day I move the sign to the next two rows. (If you forget and put the sign on the wrong row, I guarantee you will hear about it. Preadolescents and adolescents may have trouble remembering what day it is or what their assignment is, but they will never miss an opportunity to point out when something isn't fair.) Passing out the folders is a routine that helps establish consistency and teamwork, as students are responsible for preparing the class for the day. At the end of the class period, students place the folders in a plastic container that is labeled with their class period.

NOW PUT THESE THINGS IN YOUR FOLDERS, CLASS.

- **Establish a time to share.**

  This can be a time for personal anecdotes, a joke time, a time to show and comment on a YouTube™ clip, or anything else that contributes to building community relationships. This can be done at the beginning of class, with a specific time limit, or at the end of class with the same type of time frame. Be sure to set a specific time limit. Students will accept and abide by the limit if you are firm and consistent about this privilege.

- **Warm up the brain.**

  When I have a class that has trouble "settling in," I include a brain warm-up activity or journal entry to help them get their minds engaged. I have a warm-up direction or journal question ready to post as soon as the bell rings. Students start on this as soon as we have greeted one another and reviewed the agenda. I caution you to use activities or questions that matter—not just something to fill up time while you do housekeeping chores.

- **Don't let them loose!**

  Well, don't let them loose on a project, that is, without clear instructions and boundaries. If an activity involves getting supplies, you'll be asking for trouble unless you have given adequate guidance. I learned very quickly that young adolescents love to touch, push, or do just about anything except walk over and gather supplies. So, be sure to create a routine for getting supplies. You might call each row, or have one person in the row get supplies for all, or hand them out yourself, or have them pick up supplies on their way into the room. Think this through ahead of time, and you'll avoid many management problems.

● ● ● ● ● ● ● ●

Effective teachers establish limited routines to make a smooth transition to learning activities and to minimize distractions that impede learning. Inconsistency causes many young people to feel anxious and scattered.

As important as routines are, however, there is an inherent danger. I mentioned this on page 122. I'll repeat myself here: Make every effort NOT to be stale. Trust your instincts! Let surprise snatch you and students away from routine when the moment calls for it. Don't let routines squeeze out those special moments of unscheduled delight. Your middle level and high school kids can handle this. It won't rob them of security. Vow not to be the teacher type that inspired the poem by Albert Cullum, "The Geranium on the Windowsill Just Died but Teacher You Went Right On" (2000). Model the gift of spontaneity and surprise for your students.

Do you have them?
Do students "get" them?

MY EXPECTATIONS FOR A SUCCESSFUL
SIXTH GRADE EXPERIENCE ARE PLUMMETING.

Great Expectations

✔ What is one behavioral expectation in your classroom?

Why was this expectation put into place?

Is this expectation working?

How can you tell?

✔ What is one academic expectation in your classroom?

Why was this expectation put into place?

Is this expectation working?

How can you tell?

✔ What is one expectation for how a management or organizational task will be done in the classroom?

Why was this expectation put into place?

Is this expectation working?

How can you tell?

✔ What is one expectation for how a learning skill task will be done in the classroom?

Why was this expectation put into place?

Is this expectation working?

How can you tell?

✔ How were the above expectations communicated to students?

Question to parents: *What teacher behaviors do you see in classrooms where successful learning happens for your child?*

Shaun's answer: *Hands down—enthusiasm and a well disciplined classroom.*

Erik and Sara's answer: *Consistency with student expectations and guidelines; sincerity in communication with students.*

Kathryn's answer: *They have respectful classrooms. They don't have quiet classrooms, and their classrooms tend to seem chaotic to a casual observer— but a high level of respect is present to and from each individual, including the teacher.*

Cheryl's answer: *From what my five children have said over the years, I have concluded this: If my child feels that he or she has an equal chance to learn because the leader of the class, the teacher, has control over the class— then the focus of the class becomes everything the teacher does to make the subject interesting or fun.*

Expectations—this is a word that is constantly tossed about in the world of education. We're told that teachers must have high expectations for all students. School boards, administrators, state education agencies, and legislators have high expectations for teachers. Parents and community members have all sorts of expectations for teachers and for students. Teachers have expectations of parents. And what about the students? Well, they certainly have expectations too of what will happen when they sit in a classroom and live in a school. There's little doubt that expectations are omnipresent! But I am not certain that all the stakeholders in education have clear ideas about their own expectations, let alone any sort of

To implement high academic expectations, you must first have high expectations for behavior.

agreement on the list. Even more—I doubt that all of the people in this "chain of expectations" are sure how to make those expectations come to life in the classroom.

Most of the talk among educators (and parents) about "high expectations" revolves around academics. But what about expectations for behavior—where do those fit into the picture? And how do all the expectations gel together to build a caring, successful learning community?

Here's a strong bias of mine—one formed from my own experience and that of many teachers I have mentored: To implement high academic expectations, you must first have high expectations for behavior. **It cannot be the other way around.** If you want to create a rigorous curriculum where students are expected to stretch to high academic standards, then you must first concentrate on establishing a climate of high behavioral standards. Sterling academic ideals won't be useful if students do not learn processes for living and working together respectfully. Once high behavioral standards are successfully implemented, you can move with ease into working on academic excellence—and then, joyfully, watch students exceed those academic expectations!

Expectations—What and Why?

WHAT? Let's begin to get clear about what we mean by *expectations*. This noun names a huge, wide category. It covers the idea of **what?** and **how?** for everything students do in the classroom—and sometimes outside the classroom, too. This ranges from what they bring to class to how they treat each other or sharpen their pencils to how they approach their studies. When you think about it, we have dozens (maybe hundreds) of expectations for students. What gets the most attention is the expectations that adults have for the kids—how they should conduct themselves and how they should perform in the classroom. Often, adults hold these expectations closely, and students don't even fully "get" what they are. The first rule about expectations is that students must understand what they are, what they mean, and how it looks to meet them. Never assume that students, even teenagers, come to your class automatically understanding expectations for how to act in a classroom or for what it means to be a good student. Even if you have posted expectations on the wall or read them loudly and enthusiastically—do not assume students know how these translate into action.

In a classroom, expectations generally fall into these two categories:

One *Procedures*—A procedure is a set of specific steps to follow in performing a task—such as getting a hall pass, contributing to a class discussion, or putting together a report. Procedures make most of the stuff that goes on in the classroom operate more smoothly. Every classroom needs procedures for organizational tasks (such as getting and storing materials or sharpening pencils), for how we get along together (such as handling conflict, disagreeing, or behaving in discussions), for instructional tasks (such as completing

If You Can't Manage Them . . .

assignments or turning in homework), and for academic habits (such as note-taking, working hard, or doing your best). Students learn clear steps for tasks they'll do daily, and these tasks then become automatic.

Two

Rules—A rule is a principle to guide conduct. Most classrooms have at least a few rules, and they are generally connected to clearly stated consequences that ensue if the rules are not followed. Some classrooms call these *commitments*—agreements they have about how they are going to live and work with one another respectfully.

In my experience, a classroom that has reasonable, working procedures for most classroom tasks will need few rules. This is because most troubles in a classroom are the result of no procedures, inappropriate procedures, procedures that students don't fully understand, or procedures that don't work.

WHY? Clear, working expectations (rules and procedures) offer the same benefits as routines (described in Chapter 5). They offer certainty and safety. Kids know what to do and how to do it. Procedures that are discussed, explained, modeled, and practiced bring organization and smooth flow to a classroom. They help the teacher and students cultivate a climate that gives cognitive and emotional space needed for real learning.

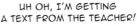

UH OH, I'M GETTING A TEXT FROM THE TEACHER!

TXTING IN CLASS IS AGNST THE RULES ☹

When expectations are put into practice, they promote responsibility and togetherness. Things work better. People get along better. Kids can feel pride in their classroom community. Many (I assure you, many!) behavior problems that might interfere with learning are eliminated or reduced.

Procedures

Follow these guidelines when you set and communicate procedures to students:

1. Make sure you outline procedures both for behavior and for academics. Consider the kinds of examples shown on page 137.

2. Procedures must be simple, reasonable, fair, and doable.

3. Each procedure must be appropriate for the developmental level of the students—this is part of the "reasonable" requirement.

4. Put them in writing for yourself and also for students—so that you can be consistent with them.

5. Procedures are worthless if students don't "get" them. Start the first day of school. Explain them thoroughly. Discuss them. Demonstrate them. Answer your students' questions about them. Talk about why you need them. SHOW them what is meant by "take your turn when contributing to classroom discussion" or "write assignments in your student planner."

If You Can't Manage Them . . .

6. Practice all procedures—right away. Try them out. Make sure they work. Practice them until they become automatic. By DOING this together, students will be improving the management of the classroom; they'll begin to take ownership of the procedures when they see how they make classroom life better.

7. Follow the procedures yourself. Don't take special liberties. Model them for students. This will show that you take them seriously. It will help students get them down pat.

8. Stop periodically to evaluate how the procedures are working. If a procedure is not working, if it is too hard to follow, or if it needs some changes, be willing to adapt it.

I have never seen peer pressure work to change student behavior. Students need an organized teacher who sets boundaries and informs them of clear expectations.
 – Cheryl, high school parent

9. Make sure you have a plan for communicating your classroom procedures to other stakeholders. (For example: How will you let parents know about homework procedures or what to do about missed assignments when a student is absent? How will you coordinate field trips with other classes?)

10. If you teach in a teaming situation, work with teammates to have consistent procedures across the team.

Sample Procedures

Procedures for Classroom Management & Organization

- Entering class
- Taking attendance
- Storing personal items
- Starting class
- Being on time
- Giving attention to teacher
- Leaving the room during class
- Arriving late at class
- Organizing supplies
- Getting and returning supplies
- Sharpening pencils
- Traveling to other places in the school
- Completing student management jobs
- Passing out papers
- Collecting papers
- Making suggestions
- Asking questions
- Sharing
- Cleaning up
- Taking home notes or papers
- Leaving class
- Resolving conflicts
- Respectful listening
- Sharing opposing viewpoints

Instructional Procedures

- Homework
- Starting on work
- Late work
- Heading on papers
- After work is completed
- Keeping track of assignments
- Extra credit
- Makeup work
- Student conferences
- Tests and quizzes
- Report cards or other reporting
- Field trips
- Special projects
- Group work
- Participation in discussions
- Keeping portfolios
- Independent studies

Learning Skills & Habits Procedures

- Contributing in class
- Communicating in class
- Note-taking
- Study skills
- Organization of learning materials
- Writing essays
- Work habits
- Completing assignments
- Self-assessments and reflections

If You Can't Manage Them . . .

Rules

Class Rules
Ms. Campbell's Class

1. Be respectful.
2. Keep the classroom blurt-free!
3. Laugh at the teacher's jokes.

Follow these guidelines when you set and communicate rules to students:

1. Carefully ponder what your rules will be. Decide ahead of time what the consequences will be for not following the rules.

2. Limit the number of rules. (An individual rule loses its power as the list grows longer.) Each one must be simple, reasonable, developmentally appropriate, and possible to follow. Students should be able to memorize them quickly. Consider the examples shown on page 141. Make sure you include rules that apply to behavior as well as to academic activity.

3. State and write each rule in language that can be understood and followed. State rules in positive terms so that students will know what to do.

4. Starting the first day, explain the rules. Be prepared to talk about the "why" of the process—why rules are needed for a group of people to live and work together, why this rule, what difference each rule makes. (Ask, "What would classroom life be like without this rule?")

5. Illustrate, demonstrate, and elaborate on each rule. Remember, your students will not automatically know what it means "to work hard," "to come to class prepared," "to be kind to others," or "to be responsible."

6. Post the rules in a prominent place.

7. Share the rules with parents and other stakeholders. Put them in your parent handbook and on your class website. When you communicate with parents, tell them why

the rules are important and what difference they will make in your classroom.

8. Starting the first day, practice the rules. Role-play the behaviors, show examples of following and not following the rules—anything to help make them habits. By DOING this together, students will be improving the management of the classroom—they'll begin to take ownership of the rules when they see how rules make classroom life better.

9. Throughout the year, keep telling and showing students how these behaviors look in the classroom. Make sure students understand that this is not something they hear on the first day of school and then forget. These will become a part of their classroom life—at all times. Practice daily. Discuss often. Continually help students see how following each of the rules translates into actual action. Ask such questions as:

    How can we tell if someone is being responsible? What are the behaviors that demonstrate this? If you are doing your best work, what does this look like?

We start with 5 rules. Mid-year, I ask students to edit them down to 3 on which to focus for the rest of the year.

– Todd, middle school teacher

10. Spell out consequences for not adhering to the rules. State these clearly and administer them consistently. See Chapter 7 for my advice on consequences and follow-through. I'll just say here that rules mean nothing if you do not follow through to help students learn them and follow them.

11. Adhere to the rules yourself. Show enthusiasm for them. Model them for students. This will show that you take them seriously. Constantly help students understand and articulate how these make life together rewarding and how they help everyone learn better.

12. If you teach in a teaming situation, work with teammates to have consistent rules and consequences across the team.

13. Your students must understand, as well, that they will be held to all the general rules of the school. Most schools have expectations about behavior on school grounds (about things such as drugs, alcohol, use of cell phones, weapons, dress codes, profanity, Internet use, and even gum-chewing). Following these is part of the expectations of your classroom.

Here's one more consideration about this process: As you consider the behaviors that are most important for (or most detrimental to) safe and successful classroom life, you will likely have some "pet peeves" in mind.

OOPS, I BLURTED!

Each of us has a right to preserve our sanity in the place where we spend many hours each day. I suggest to teachers that they answer this question: "What three behaviors, if you could eliminate them, would inspire you to want to teach seven days a week?" The top one on my list is "blurting" (interrupting, speaking out of turn, or interjecting something irrelevant when someone else is talking). This drives me nuts! Even though this falls under another rule—"Be respectful"—I single it out and have a separate rule about it because it is such a pattern for middle school kids, and I feel it needs special emphasis. You might think about your own list of three behaviors that are not negotiable in your classroom!

Sample Rules

Expectations
Respect each other.
Respect yourself.
Support each other.
Learn everything you can.

Rules
1. Be respectful.
2. Be responsible.
3. Be prepared.

As a member of this class,
I agree to . . .
  treat every other person with respect.
  do my work, and try my hardest.

We Will . . .
  Be kind.
  Do our work.
  Try hard.

Shared Expectations
Be on time.
Be prepared.
Respect yourself,
others, and
all property.

COMMITMENTS TO EACH OTHER
Every student and all opinions are respected.
No one is ridiculed.
There is no touching without permission.
We will speak in kind, appropriate voices.

If You Can't Manage Them . . .

Academic Expectations

Let's get back to the topic of academic expectations. School is about learning. It's our job as teachers to know our students' learning styles and abilities and help them reach their potential and stretch beyond.

As I said earlier, there is little chance that they will meet high standards if their school environment is chaotic or unsafe. Clear behavioral and procedural expectations (I repeat myself!) provide the safety that sets minds free to soar! Once you have the framework in place for a functional, well-managed setting where students know what to do and how to get along, you can focus on actions to move students academically, to challenge their thinking, inspire their desire to learn, and help them achieve their highest potential.

High academic expectations start with the teacher's belief in every student.

In my view, high academic expectations start (and finish) with the teacher's belief in every student. The teacher must believe (and show that belief) that all students can learn, grow, and excel.

- **Students must be sure that YOU believe they can learn**—and can do things that are even harder than they might think they can do. If they do not know this unequivocally—you can forget about high standards. Well, some of your students may be intrinsically motivated already—but even those kids need your belief. You will show your belief in them (or lack of it) by your comments, attitudes, behaviors, tone of voice, responses to them, gestures, facial expressions, body language, enthusiasm for learning, preparedness, lessons, and energy.

- **You must teach students what high standards are.** What does "high" mean? It means to succeed at everything you possibly can. It means to accomplish, master, understand, and do tasks, concepts, and processes at your grade level and beyond—or beyond what you are used to doing. You teach them by **showing** the difference between low and high standards.

- **You must teach students how to reach high standards.** This means a lot of showing and talking. Talk about the following behaviors and discuss what they look like in school. Give examples of success and failure. Watch for these behaviors. Affirm the successes. Keep on top of this constantly. (A caution about the following list: Teachers say things like this to students all the time. This is not just a list of things to say. I guarantee—these are the kinds of statements that go in one ear and out the other.) Help them "get" what it means to be a student, and to be a successful student. I repeat—you must show students precisely what each of these components of "high standards" looks like:

Be prepared.
Do your work.
Do your work well.
Do all your work.
Do your work on time.
Take homework seriously.
Turn in your homework.
Try hard.
Put forth effort.
Bring all your supplies to class.
Be ready to learn.
Study for tests.
Welcome feedback.
Listen.
Participate.
Share your ideas.
Finish what you start.
Reflect on your work.
Make good decisions.
Push yourself beyond the easy.
Don't settle for mediocre work.
Try new things.
Ask for help.

JOHN SAYS HIS DOG ALWAYS EATS HIS HOMEWORK.

IS THAT TRUE?

WELL, HIS DOG JUST GRADUATED FROM HARVARD.

• • • • **Don't sit down. Keep moving.** Keep on top of the students' work and progress. I don't have a desk. I am constantly among my students—always paying attention to how they are doing, who is lost, who needs a push, who needs a scaffold.

• • • • **Model high expectations.** Have high expectations for yourself. Demonstrate in the way you do your job every behavior you try to teach them about academic standards.

Expectations for the Teacher

Here is the first expectation for the teacher—that he or she believes that students can reach high standards. Hundreds of research studies verify the transformative effects of the teacher's expectations for student growth. In his classic examination of leadership, Warren Bennis (1994) found that the high expectations of teachers for their students was, alone, sufficient to cause an increase of 25 points in student IQ scores. This is not just a call to some philosophical idea. It is not enough to say you believe all students can learn and excel. Look at every one of your students and say that (and believe it) about him or her. Treat all students consistently and equitably.

Tune in. Show up. So far in this book, I have been adamant about being tuned in to yourself and your students as human beings. You can't promote good learning, teach acceptable behavior, run an orderly classroom, or teach content effectively without being present to your students—without the relationships, respect, and procedures discussed in Chapters 1 through 6.

> What kinds of teachers have best helped my child learn? Teachers with clear expectations for the students and clear expectations for themselves.
>
> – Greg, middle school parent

Be committed to teaching an academic course of study—and teach it well. I am just as adamant about this part of the teacher's role. This is what the job of a teacher is. Create an academic environment that says, "We are here to learn. I believe you can learn. I am here to help you." When Warren Bennis reported the astounding effects of high teacher expectations, he made it clear that high standards must be accompanied by supports necessary to help students reach

If You Can't Manage Them . . .

them. The absence of this, he said, "would not only be ludicrous but cruel and frustrating, robbing students of their intrinsic motivation for learning" (1994, pg 45).

Set high behavioral and academic expectations for yourself. Be prepared. Be on time. Be enthusiastic. Stretch yourself. Students must see you epitomizing a good learner. Don't let yourself or your lessons get stale. Be consistent. Come to school every day (from the first day) assuming that learning will take place. Start class on time. Every time—give your students a clear message that this class is so important that we will get underway right away—as soon as the bell rings! Support, demonstrate, and enforce all behavioral expectations.

• • • • • • • •

I want to help teachers (including myself) consider what it means to have high expectations for behavior and academics within their classrooms. Return to page 130 at the beginning of the chapter. Review what you wrote about your current expectations. Pay attention to the ones you said were working. Think about why those are working. This is your starting point for developing other rules and procedures that work.

I have tried to identify characteristics and behaviors of teachers who have high expectations and help students meet them. To conclude this chapter, I offer two self-reflections based on my discoveries about these characteristics and behaviors. I use these at several points throughout the year to help myself focus on setting and modeling high expectations. One focuses on expectations for behavior; the other focuses on academic expectations. You will find these on pages 147 through 150.

Self-Reflection: Behavior Expectations, pg 1

Do I demonstrate high behavioral expectations for my students?

Rate yourself on each statement: 0 (Never Do) to 5 (Always Do)

___ I start class on time, sending a clear message that this class is important and setting the expectation that the students will be ready.

___ I set and communicate clear behavioral expectations. I make sure that students fully understand what each expectation means.

___ My students know definitively what the consequences of misbehavior will be.

___ I apply consequences consistently and equitably.

___ When I confront a student about a behavioral issue, the student always has a chance to tell his or her side of the story.

___ I redirect students who blurt, talk when someone else is talking, or speak in a tone that would be considered disrespectful.

___ I do not use "shh" to quiet or redirect the class. Instead I use the student's name, proximity, and "I need" statements.

___ I teach appropriate behavior instead of using "Knock it off" or "Stop that" (for example: eyes on me, pencils down, mouths closed, knees facing me).

___ I am deliberate in building relationships with all my students. (For example, I greet students at door, smile, laugh, share personal tidbits, ask students about things they have shared.)

continues on next page

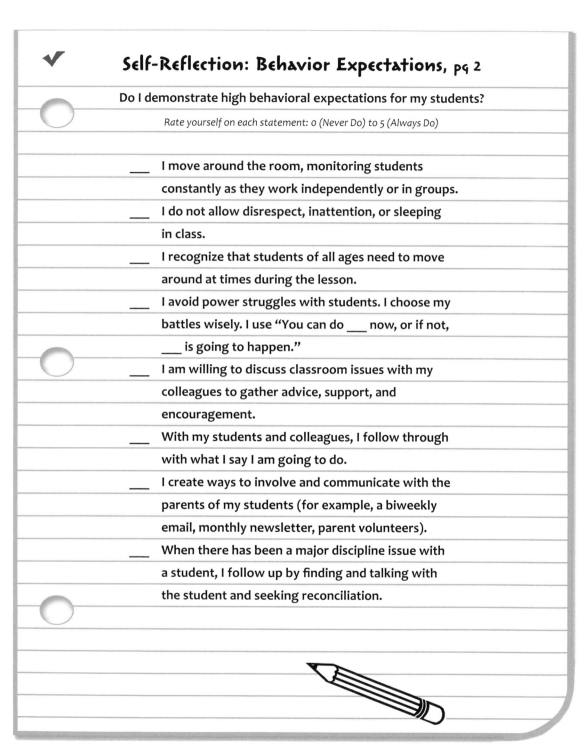

Self-Reflection: Behavior Expectations, pg 2

Do I demonstrate high behavioral expectations for my students?

Rate yourself on each statement: 0 (Never Do) to 5 (Always Do)

___ I move around the room, monitoring students constantly as they work independently or in groups.

___ I do not allow disrespect, inattention, or sleeping in class.

___ I recognize that students of all ages need to move around at times during the lesson.

___ I avoid power struggles with students. I choose my battles wisely. I use "You can do ___ now, or if not, ___ is going to happen."

___ I am willing to discuss classroom issues with my colleagues to gather advice, support, and encouragement.

___ With my students and colleagues, I follow through with what I say I am going to do.

___ I create ways to involve and communicate with the parents of my students (for example, a biweekly email, monthly newsletter, parent volunteers).

___ When there has been a major discipline issue with a student, I follow up by finding and talking with the student and seeking reconciliation.

Self-Reflection: Academic Expectations, pg 1

Do I demonstrate high academic expectations for my students?

Rate yourself on each statement: 0 (Never Do) to 5 (Always Do)

___ I truly believe ALL students can learn and succeed in my classroom.

___ I have high expectations for myself as a teacher; I reflect on my lessons and teaching; I am willing to try new ideas and strategies; and I am an advocate for my profession.

___ I create an essential question for every unit and make sure each lesson attempts to answer that question.

___ I have my agenda and goal of the lesson posted in my classroom for students to see. I review this daily with students.

___ I implement STOP (Stop Teaching—Observe Progress) or other ways to monitor my students' progress every 10 to 15 minutes throughout the lesson.

___ I incorporate the following rule in my teaching: Review new material every 10 minutes, again 48 hours later, and again 7 days later (Eric Jensen, *Top 10 Brain-Based Teaching Strategies, 2010*).

___ I create opportunities in my class for students to speak with one another and the entire class—for example, TAPS (Think Aloud Problem Solve) or Socratic Seminar.

___ I incorporate WICRT (Writing, Inquiry, Collaboration, Reading, & Technology) into most of my lessons (from AVID, Advancement Via Individual Determination).

___ I provide timely feedback on my students' tests, assignments, quizzes, and projects.

___ I recognize my own learning style and tendencies and try to develop lessons that incorporate other methods of instruction.

continues on next page

If You Can't Manage Them . . .

Self-Reflection: Academic Expectations, pg 2

Do I demonstrate high academic expectations for my students?

Rate yourself on each statement: 0 (Never Do) to 5 (Always Do)

___ I do not blame the parents of my students for their lack of homework completion, engagement, or behavior. Instead, I try to meet each student where he or she is, and work from there.

___ I attempt to incorporate current relevant information into my lessons and allow students to discuss the topic being presented (current events, YouTube™ clips, and such).

___ I utilize Bloom's Taxonomy to develop questions for assignments as well as for class discussions.

___ I am very purposeful in the homework I assign. I may even state the purpose of the assignment on the homework.

___ I recognize that it is my job to help students reach the high expectations I have established. I provide help, time, and resources, before or after school, to help all students succeed.

___ I use exit cards to make sure students understand the material or to determine if they have questions.

___ I find ways to hold students accountable for what has been taught each day in my class by implementing daily quizzes, active votes, clickers, or reflection writing.

___ To have an understanding of the levels within my class, I know the state scores in reading and math for each of my students.

___ I recognize that I must first establish high behavioral expectations prior to implementing high academic standards.

Chapter 7

Consequences & Follow-Through

Say what will happen and make it happen.

MRS. BROWN ALWAYS GIVES
A STERN WARNING FOR THE FIRST TARDY.
SECOND TARDY, SHE THREATENS TO TELL YOUR PARENTS;
THIRD TARDY, SHE THREATENS TO TELL THE PRINCIPAL;
FOURTH TARDY, SHE GIVES A STERN WARNING.

GET THROUGH THE FIRST THREE, AND YOU'RE HOME FREE!

Speak and Deliver

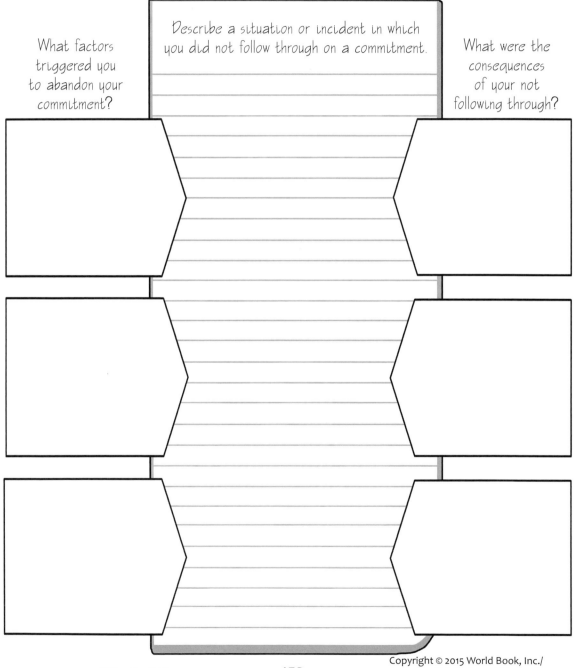

What factors triggered you to abandon your commitment?

Describe a situation or incident in which you did not follow through on a commitment.

What were the consequences of your not following through?

I'm having a flashback to 1997. I was teaching 7th grade geography to a room of thirty-five students—plus Mark. Let's just say that having Mark in class was like adding five more hyperactive middle school kids to one small room. I think I redirected Mark once every five minutes. It was not long before I realized that he was taking more time and energy from me than all the other students combined. Something had to be done! And I knew that that something had to start with me. As I drove home one night, I reflected on Mark, what he was doing, and how I was handling the situation. What was I doing wrong?

Two things hit me: I was not following through on the consequences I issued; and the consequences I had created were unrealistic. For example, I said things like this: "Mark, if you don't stop doing what you're doing, you are never coming back into the class," or "Mark, if you don't get with the program, I'm having your mother come in to class and sit with you."

These were not reasonable consequences. They, like some others I had grabbed out of the air, were nearly impossible to enforce. Mark quickly learned that I wasn't serious—that I was not going to enforce the consequences. Therefore, every day for a (brutal) 88-minute block, I had no handle on Mark or the situation.

The number one mistake teachers make in addressing behavioral problems is NOT following through with the consequence they have established. (This is particularly true of new teachers, but it is a huge problem for teachers at many levels of experience.) Of course, this is just part of the whole picture of teacher response. Students must know exactly what behaviors are unacceptable in the first place (and why), what acceptable behavior looks like, and what will happen when rules are broken. Teachers must set clear, reasonable, and enforceable consequences for breaches of rules or protocols. There must be a process for

> The number one mistake teachers make is NOT following through with the consequence they have issued.

If You Can't Manage Them . . .

enforcing and following up on the consequences, and for resolving the issues and reconciling after bruised feelings. But, of all possible responses to misbehavior, follow-through is the one most frequently botched (or avoided) by teachers.

In this chapter, I want to pass on to you what I've learned (in some cases, the hard way!) about consequences and follow-through. I'll share some approaches that work when rules or procedures are broken or disregarded. We'll look at . . .

- which actions or behaviors really are "problems"
- how to prevent problems for most of the students
- how to set reasonable consequences
- how to tell students what the consequences are
- which actions to take when rules are not followed
- what it means to "follow through" and how to do it
- how to resolve issues after the consequence is applied
- how to reconcile with students you've had to discipline

The 80%–15%–5% Rule

In their book *Discipline with Dignity*, researchers Curwin and Mendler suggest that most classrooms are comprised of three groups of students. About 80% of the students rarely break rules or violate principles. The second group—about 15% of the class—are students who push the limits or break rules on a somewhat regular basis. The final 5% are chronic rule breakers and are somewhat out of control most of the time. The task for a teacher, the authors assert, is to manage the 15% without alienating or over-regulating the 80% and without backing the 5% into a corner. They recommend that teachers focus on preventing discipline problems for the first two groups, while having a plan for handling the serious issues that arise related to the chronic rule-breakers (1988).

> As a proud middle school teacher of 18 years, I couldn't agree more! I find that Curwin and Mendler are right on about the 80%–15%–5% split! There will always be that 5% to constantly redirect, confront, and at times remove from your classroom. Even the best classroom managers will struggle with that 5%. I agree that we all need a plan for handling the 5%, but I would add that we need a clear process for responding to the 15% to keep minor issues from becoming major.

Any plan for handling the serious issues or even less serious issues is built around clearly defined expectations and consequences for not meeting them. And the key part of that plan is follow-through on consequences—one of the most critical factors in effective classroom management.

If you can't follow through—don't issue the consequence. Each of your students will soon figure out that you do not have the courage, ability, or will to follow through and that your threats are only that—threats. Ultimately (trust me, this does not take long), students lose respect for you. Then the undesirable behaviors continue and often escalate.

BRINGING MARK'S MOTHER TO CLASS EVERY DAY WAS NOT AN EFFECTIVE SOLUTION TO THE PROBLEM.

If You Can't Manage Them . . .

What is even more damaging is that the 15% of the students who Curwin and Mendler describe as "sitting on the fence" are watching. Who? They are watching YOU to see how you handle those students who create most of the problems. (Do you ignore them, allow them to speak disrespectfully, engage them, follow through?) If they see that you do not follow through, they lose faith in your ability to lead the class. With lightning speed, their adolescent brains process this and tell them, "Hey! Let's join the party!" (Then do the math: Your 5% problem has exploded into a 20% problem.) This 15% is a critical group. (I know this, because I was one of this 15%. As soon as I saw the teacher waffle, I was over the fence!) As the leader of the classroom, you must make sure these students are on your side of the fence.

Define and Avoid Problems

My strongest message in this chapter is that it's a big mistake not to follow through. But first, you must ask: "Just what is it on which I am following through?"

Before you can set consequences and consider responses to problems in the classroom, you must be clear (for yourself and your students) what the behaviors are that warrant consequences.

There is a host of ways students can disregard, forget, push limits on, or outright challenge many classroom processes and procedures. But many of these are not the big issues of discipline. Most misbehaviors (such as showing off at the pencil sharpener, coming to class late, talking out of turn, snickering during lessons, stumbling clumsily about the classroom, not paying attention), while annoying, are not flagrant or malicious violations of classroom rules. These are things that can and should be addressed with stronger teacher direction or presence, more practice, and more behavior instruction.

Some irritations in the classroom are normal outcomes of the physical and emotional developmental level of the students. Preadolescents and adolescents slouch, squirm, flail arms around, make annoying noises, and such. Some of these things will become problems only if you give attention to them. You might think about which behaviors are best ignored!

> Management Advice to the Teacher:
>
> Be assertive.
>
> – Haviland, grade 7

Define inappropriate behavior—for yourself and your students. This is part of the process you must set in motion when you identify classroom rules and teach students about respect. (See Chapters 3 and 6.) What have you made clear to students? What have you taught them? Remember that holding students to expectations begins with effective teaching of the expectations. As I emphasized in Chapter 6—be sure you have given plenty of time to effective social and behavioral instruction so students know what appropriate and inappropriate behavior looks like.

If you remember all the way back to Chapter 1, I gave you a long list of some things teachers do to cause problems in the classroom. That was followed by a long list of ways to prevent problems. You can refer back to those pages for a refresher course on avoiding problems.

Here are four reminders to help as you review this important task of avoiding problems in the first place:

One   *Double-check the classroom system.*

Much misbehavior is the fault of the classroom system—room arrangement, lack of procedures, lack of training in procedures, or lax organization. Deter a host of behavioral issues with good teaching of rules and procedures, consistent preparation, careful classroom organization, and constant engagement of students in meaningful learning activities.

Two   *Reinforce behavior that is appropriate.*

Many teachers forget about this. The misbehavior is such a focus that we often forget to pay attention to what is going right. Notice and affirm the appropriate behavior before students have a chance to do it wrong.

Three   *Work to preserve dignity.*

I find that many students who chronically misbehave do so when they feel their personal dignity is assaulted, when they feel hopeless about their academic ability, or when they are socially or emotionally humiliated. All students are more likely to lose motivation to behave well when they perceive they are not valued. An affront to dignity is a recipe for stirring up trouble. Actually, it is a healthy sign for students to fight for their dignity! Help them do this appropriately. Start by awarding them dignity privately, and in front of their peers.

Four *Grow eyes in the back of your head.*

In Chapter 1, I listed this as one of the strategies for avoiding problems in the classroom. Back in the 1970's, researcher Jacob Kounin came up with another way to describe this brilliant teacher technique. During his observations of classroom management, he coined the word "withitness" to describe a feature of teachers who successfully prevented misbehavior. This term referred to constant awareness of what is occurring in the classroom. He found that a teacher with this talent could suppress misbehaviors of students who were starting trouble, identify which problem occurring in the classroom was the most serious and deal with that first, and refocus an off-task student before the behavior got out of hand.

"Withitness" is constant awareness of what is occurring in the classroom.

If You Can't Manage Them . . .

Set Clear Consequences

If you have rules and expectations for behavior (which you should!), there must be predetermined consequences that will follow if the expectations are not met. And you must follow through with the consequences. It's that simple. It doesn't matter what your teaching style is or your personality, or how long you have been teaching. Expectations must be accompanied by consequences that actually get enforced.

Thus, when you set consequences, make sure that . . .
- they are reasonable
- they are correlated to the students' developmental level
- they do not diminish the student's dignity
- they are enforceable
- the students know what they are
- students know ALL the possible consequences
- you do not make them up on the spot
- students understand why this consequence is used
- the consequences escalate with repeated offenses

What Are Consequences?

These will differ for different teachers, even for different groups of students in different years. You'll have to set your own list and progression, but here are examples of some used by other teachers:
- reminding
- redirecting
- verbal warning

- sent to the hallway for a few minutes followed by talk with the teacher
- other kind of timeout or isolation
- removal of privileges
- 10 minutes of silent lunch
- lunch detention with the teacher
- behavior contracts
- sent to the office (principal, dean, etc.)
- call to parents
- conference with parents and student
- in-school suspension
- community service
- out-of-school suspension
- expulsion

My usual progression is:

- one redirection or reminder with description of consequence that will ensue if the behavior is repeated
- the second time for the same behavior: into the hallway for a few minutes, then I talk with the student to discuss and remind him or her of the appropriate behavior and consequences
- send to office
- call parents
- in-school suspension
- out-of-school suspension
- expulsion

If You Can't Manage Them . . .

Note: By the way, you might also create a list of consequences for appropriate behavior, too, such as:

- extra free time in class
- extended lunch period
- lunch or snack coupons
- homework pass
- extra time with technology, such as a computer

Take Action

• • • • If you don't take action in response to an inappropriate or rule-breaking behavior, then your efforts are wasted. On the first offense . . .

1. Respond quickly.
2. Use a calm, soft voice.
3. Do not speak in anger.
4. Make direct eye contact.
5. Acknowledge appropriate behavior if some is evident.
6. Give your verbal warning or redirection.
7. Remind student of the inappropriateness of the behavior.
8. Remind student of the rule.
9. If your system is to give only one warning, state at this time what the choice is: "You may refrain from doing this again, or you will be separated from your friends in the study room."
10. Move near the student to help her or him gain control.

- - - - If you have given your one (or other predetermined number) verbal warning, reminder, and redirection—and the behavior continues . . .

> If you can't follow through— don't issue the consequence.

1. Act quickly.
2. Use a calm, soft voice.
3. Do not speak in anger.
4. Make direct eye contact.
5. Do not threaten.
6. Do not give a second chance.
7. State what the inappropriate behavior is.
8. State the consequence.
9. Do not negotiate or allow excuses.
10. Do not humiliate.
11. Implement the consequence right away.

- - - - When applying the consequence, find a time to talk with the student as soon as possible, and . . .

1. Identify what the student has done.
2. Describe the appropriate behavior.
3. Let the student talk. Help her or him explain why the behavior is not okay.
4. Keep the same direct, calm, unemotional tone.
5. Separate the inappropriate behavior from the person.
6. Explain and discuss the consequence.
7. Enforce the consequence fairly.

If You Can't Manage Them . . .

8. Examine the circumstances. This may help you find ways to keep this behavior or incident from repeating.

9. If you plan to contact the parent(s), tell the student.

In any incident where you confront a student and enforce consequences, remember . . .

- that it is not the severity, but the consistency, of response that affects student behavior.

- that even in discipline situations, students must feel their dignity and autonomy is respected.

- to pay attention to your own demeanor (tone and volume of voice, word choice, body language, emotions) so that as you hold students to expectations, you do so in a spirit that preserves your relationship with the student and promotes your goal of teaching each one to manage his or her own behavior.

But Follow-Through Is So Hard!

For the past several years, I have worn the hat of district mentor for new teachers. In this role, I have had dozens of chances to observe and discuss follow-through (or lack of it) with my new teachers. At one of our meetings, a new teacher admitted that her biggest barrier to managing her classroom was her lack of follow-through.

"Great!" I thought, "This is one step in the right direction—recognizing and naming the problem!"

I was curious as to why, if she knew that lack of follow-through was standing in the way of her success and sanity, it was still an issue for her. So I asked her, "Why do you let follow-through get in the way?"

She looked me straight in the eye and said, "I'm afraid if I follow through with consequences, they won't like me."

I strongly recommend that you do not EVER "friend" your students on any social network.

I looked around the room, and saw that all the new teachers in the group were nodding their heads in agreement. I knew at this moment that we had work to do.

This is a mistake many of us make in our early teaching careers—assuming that students won't like us if we hold them to expectations. (Any wise reader here knows well that this is not just a problem for new teachers!)

Here's my response to this: First of all, I hope you have friends that are your age. If you do not have friends, I highly recommend you look to Match.com® before you ever consider befriending your students!

Secondly, you must drop this belief that if you don't follow through and hold them to consequences, your students will like you more, which in turn will reduce behavioral problems. This will not happen! This mindset will lead to chaos inside your classroom. When students

If You Can't Manage Them . . .

see that you are a pushover, do not follow through, and continue to issue idle threats—it is only a matter of time before students will try to take advantage of you, and maybe like you even less.

You want students to respect you, not like you. Trust me, most students want you to follow through, want you to be the leader of the classroom, and truly want to learn. Once students know that you mean what you say, respect will follow, and you will be surprised at how many students will like you.

This never fails: Toward the end of every school year, at least one or two students will ask if they can call me Kim. I always respond, "Only my friends call me Kim, and right now you are my students, not my friends. Maybe someday when you are much older you can call me Kim."

I have also been asked several times to befriend my current and former students on Facebook™. I never agree to do this. I strongly recommend that you do not "friend" your students on any social network. To be their friends and share private information on a social network is taking a huge risk. If you want to create a Facebook™ page or group for school academic or club purposes, knock yourself out! This is appropriate.

Management Advice to Teachers:
Be an adult. Once you get too chummy, kids will take advantage of you forever.
– Brett, grade 9

Wanting to be liked by students is a powerful deterrent to follow-through. But it is not the only one. In Chapter 1, I wrote about many personal styles, factors, influences, and experiences that affect the way you respond to students—particularly when

misbehavior or conflict is involved. There are other fears and factors that come into play in that moment when you choose to confront, or not to confront, clear rule violations. Go back to page 152 and review your response to the exercise "Speak and Deliver." Consider the factors that you listed. Consider the consequences of not following through that you listed. This may help to increase your understanding of difficulties you have with follow-through.

Help with Follow-Through

Students must face the consequences for their actions, but those consequences need to be scaffolded so the child has an opportunity to change the behavior and remain in class. Now, I want to assert that if the behavior is extreme (such as fighting, absolute refusal to follow directions, or other severe outbursts), you need to ignore the scaffolding and immediately remove the child from the classroom. However, when behavior is less severe and interrupts learning, apply tactics that will lead to behavior change.

Today, as an experienced teacher, with a student like Mark (see page 153), my redirection may sound something like this: "Mark, I need you to sit down. Thank you."

If Mark finds himself in other trouble, my second redirection would sound something like this, "Mark, I have already redirected you once today. This will be my last redirection or you will be in the hall." You will notice that on the second redirection, I am very specific with what I will do with Mark if this happens again. Now, I MUST put him in the hall if it happens again.

If you state possible consequences or choices of behavior and do not follow through when the student chooses to continue the negative behavior—you've got more trouble. Your non-action sends a message to students that they don't have to worry about consequences. All of the students have just witnessed you, as the classroom leader, not holding Mark accountable. If Mark has chosen to do the right thing, then give him a compliment. Always be explicit as to why he is getting a compliment. For example, if Mark handles a transition without incident you may say, "Mark, that was great. You didn't touch, push, or make faces. You are a rock star. Nice work."

Because follow-through is so important (and because so many teachers struggle with this), I offer five strategies to consider when you have a student like Mark.

One

Take time to reflect.

Many times, when a classroom feels chronically disrupted, the teacher thinks it is due to all the kids who are acting out. When I work with teachers who are struggling with a particular class, I always ask them to reflect and name the three to five students they think are causing the most trouble.

To help get at the ringleaders of the class, a question I pose is, "If you could get rid of three to five students, who would they be?" Teachers can immediately answer, and usually we quickly find and name the true instigators of most of the trouble within their classrooms. Once the leaders are identified, we can begin to put a plan into place. It is important to recognize that more than likely it is a few (5%) of the students who are wreaking havoc. So, take the time to reflect. Narrow it down to who is starting and encouraging the chaos. Then focus your attention, your quick confrontation, and your consequences on those individuals.

Two

Plan ahead.

If you have a classroom with several students who are disruptive, have your plan for response worked out before class starts. For example, if you have a Quiet Room or an In-School Suspension room, notify those

If You Can't Manage Them . . .

teachers or staff members in charge of that room that you may be sending a few students their direction that day or week. Many times in my career, I have used my prep period to speak to individual students about what I expect of them and what the consequence will be if their misbehavior continues during our next class. As I greet students at the door, I always make sure that I remind those individuals about our earlier conversation.

Three *Find time to talk to the troublesome student.*

If you have not had time to talk to the identified students during a prep period or after school, try to catch each one before class starts. Explain that you will only redirect them once and then they will be sent to the office (or whatever your next step is). Trust me, that child you spoke to will test you immediately! Remember, you haven't followed through before. So in the student's mind, today will not be any different. Surprise the student! For the love of Pete . . . DO WHAT YOU SAY YOU ARE GOING TO DO . . . SEND HIM OR HER TO THE OFFICE, HALL, WHEREVER! Others will get the message.

Four *Choose consequences thoughtfully.*

What can you live with? What is realistic? What progression will you use? Will you start with one redirection? Is your second redirection to send the student into the hall? Is your third redirection to send the student to the office and make a call home? Establish this progression while you are calm. And as I have said earlier, make sure your students know the progression and know for sure that you will follow that progression. If you are new to a school, speak to a colleague or the assistant principal to make sure you are clear on what the progression is for your particular school.

Most educational experts will tell you that if you are redirecting individual students more than twice a class period, it is too much and you are not being effective as a classroom manager.

Think about this: If you are about to issue Mark his third redirection, you are working much harder than you need to regarding Mark's behavior. It is time to find another consequence or goal for Mark. Managing preadolescents or adolescents in the heat of the moment can be very difficult and not productive for anyone involved. Alleviate the difficulty, mistakes, and mishandling by planning ahead.

Five

Follow up after enforcing consequences.

When you do end up sending the student to the office or other in-school accommodation, make contact with that student before the next class. The student has experienced a difficult encounter. Now she or he is not sure if you will hold a grudge, still be mad, or want to dish out some punishment the next day. To the adolescent brain, it now could be: me (student) versus you (teacher).

It is well worth your time and energy (and so important to the child) to find that student during your prep period and have a conversation about what happened the class or day before. Allow enough time

If You Can't Manage Them . . .

to pass for you and the student to calm down. Also, be sure you know how you want to approach the student, and what you want out of the conversation. If you truly value relationships, then this is one of those moments where you need to **act** on building that relationship. If you feel the conversation with this student would be too difficult, ask your administrator to mediate your discussion.

Resolve and Reconcile

Please, I beg you, do not just carry on with business as usual after a consequence-enforcing incident! If you do, you will have chipped away at the relationship you worked so hard to build. You will also miss a wonderful teaching opportunity.

Remember that your long-term goal is for students to be able to make wise decisions inside and outside of school. You want them to become caring, responsible problem-solvers. You want them to understand that their choices have consequences—and move toward more frequent choices that produce healthy consequences for them and others. This means that they need practice making choices and mistakes in a safe environment.

The purpose for consequences is to teach students that behavior produces effects. Application of consequences must be instructive. This means that you must handle student misbehavior in ways that make sense, provide for communication and nurture, and teach alternative, appropriate behavior. You can't accomplish this purpose if you apply a sterile consequence without further connection right away. So, as I said in my fifth bit of advice (section above), find time to reconcile and reconnect—to keep the relationship alive, support the student, and provide new skills for better behavior.

Even with the first offense, let the student know you believe she or he can behave better. With more serious offenses, find more time to . . .

- connect about what happened
- give the student a chance to talk
- make a plan for future behavior
- provide support to the student for future efforts
- tell the student that the next day or next class offers a fresh start and that you will not be holding grudges

And here's some more good news! When you handle one student's misbehavior in a clean, straightforward manner that enforces well-explained, reasonable consequences—there is a wonderful side benefit. That student and all the other students get a great lesson in why the behavior was unacceptable. They see logical consequences for the behavior. They feel the safety of an adult who helps them work toward responsible

If You Can't Manage Them . . .

actions. They see the aftermath that includes a continued caring relationship. And the classmates are less likely to imitate the inappropriate behavior. I know this from experience! Your wise follow-through teaches great lessons to (and results in better behavior from) your whole class. But (and this is big!)—the follow-through must be consistent. Intermittent follow-through is perhaps even more harmful than none at all!

Your wise follow-through teaches great lessons to, and results in better behavior from, your entire class.

Behavioral Rubrics Are Your Friends

Behavioral rubrics have been good friends to me in my management efforts. These have helped me and my students monitor and modify behavior. Make rubrics your friends, too.

• • • • What Is a Behavioral Rubric?

A rubric is a performance-based assessment that rates the quality of student work or behavior using a scoring guide. Rubrics are set up in a variety of ways, for a variety of purposes. They can be highly customized to your needs.

Some teachers choose to create a holistic rubric that rates a variety of characteristics related to behavior. I like to use a rubric to identify a certain category of behavior and then specify certain actions that characterize that behavior. Some teachers do the scoring on the rubrics. I prefer a rubric that is self-scored by the student. I feel this is a great tool for increasing student involvement and decision making surrounding his or her own behavior.

Here are some specific areas within the whole scope of appropriate behavior. These are the kinds of topics on which I might develop rubrics:

- taking responsibility
- respecting classmates and staff members
- classroom participation
- being prepared
- concern for learning
- listening
- attention
- conflict
- following directions
- managing impulsivity
- striving to do one's best
- assignment completion

What Are the Benefits?

I included this topic in the consequences chapter because I find the use of rubrics to be a great help for kids who have trouble controlling their behavior. In addition, rubrics nicely support efforts to extend the teachings that accompany consequences and efforts to resolve behavioral issues after consequences are applied.

Management Advice to Teachers:
Talk calmly. Warn students about behavior. Don't allow students to talk back to you.
– Paige, grade 7

When students help to design or use a self-scoring rubric . . .

- immediately, they are involved in examining their own behavior
- they take ownership of the topic of their behavior
- they are given voice in assessing their own behavior
- they have, before their eyes, a reminder of what acceptable behavior looks like
- their positive behavior is affirmed with points
- they have to think about questions such as:
  "What did I do?"
  "What is the problem?"
  "What should I do next time?"
- they are focused on preventing misbehavior
- the completion of and sharing of the completed rubric gives a great opportunity for student-teacher discussion, connection, and resolution

As a teacher, I get to see what students are thinking about their behavior. It is another form of feedback to me. The rubrics help me start discussions with them. The rubrics give me tools for discussions with parents. And best of all, student behavior improves when I use rubrics!

How Do Rubrics Work?

The idea of a rubric is that a score is assigned to different levels or descriptions of behavior regarding a topic. For example, if a student is scoring herself on responsibility, there could be a rating of 4 to 1, meaning:

4—characteristics of a highly responsible student,

3—characteristics observable in a student who is responsible with a few exceptions,

2—description of a student who needs improvement in responsibility, and

1—description of a student taking so little responsibility that classroom performance is seriously impeded.

The descriptors in the rubric are specific. A student or adult can read the criteria and easily decide what score to give. You can use these in whatever way you wish— with a few students or many students. You can discuss the finished rubrics individually with students. You can ask students to add written comments. You can devise individual rubrics for individual students' needs.

When I design a behavior rubric, I first think about what motivates my students—in particular that 15% of students who frequently misbehave (or the 15% plus the 5% of chronic rule-breakers). I ask myself if this group is more motivated by academic or social rewards. If they are more academically motivated, then I design a rubric with which they can earn points to enter into their grading program. This increases responsibility for their behavior and gives them a topic to discuss with their parents who see the additional points. Basically, these are easy points for doing what they are supposed to do.

However, if students are more socially motivated, or if most members of the class need work in a particular area, I might create a rubric that involves the entire class.

If You Can't Manage Them . . .

I might create a rubric that seeks to reduce the blurting, talking out of turn, or wandering from the study group during work time. I might break the class time into two thirty-minute chunks. At the end of that time, students complete a rubric on this topic. Students rate themselves on whether they refrained from blurting out or talking when someone else was talking, and whether they stayed with the group during work time. If a certain number of points is gained, the class earns a 3-minute break to socialize or play a game.

If you try this, have a backup plan to deal with any students who deliberately sabotage the plan. This might include pulling them out, sending them into the hall, or "loaning" them for a while to another teacher on your team.

Management Advice to Teachers:

Don't keep giving warning after warning. Just follow through!

– Sadie and Michael, middle school students

Do not do this type of rubric for points that add to their grades, as this can become punishment to all students for the noncooperation of a few. Students and parents will give tremendous push-back for this idea, and it is unfair to the group.

As I said, there are countless kinds of rubrics and ways to use them. The next two pages show some examples of rubrics created for isolated behavioral skills areas. Use these as models or inspiration to create your own. Engage students in the process. This will increase their voice and ownership in managing their own behavior.

Appropriate Verbal Participation

Name _____ Class Period _____ Date(s) _____

	Always 2 pts	Mostly 1 pt	Rarely 0 pts
I was able to keep from blurting during class.			
I refrained from talking when the teacher or my peers were talking.			
I raised my hand and waited to be called on to speak.			
I listened respectfully when others were speaking.			

_____ points (of 8 pts)

If fewer than 6 points, provide your phone number: _____

RESPECT

Name _____

Class Period _____ Date(s) _____

	Always 2 pts	Mostly 1 pt	Rarely 0 pts
I listened to my peers and respected their opinions.			
I refrained from using abusive language.			
I respected all property of others.			
I cooperated with peers and the teachers.			
I responded kindly and appropriately to peers and teachers.			
I listened to teachers and followed directions.			

_____ points (of 12 pts)

If fewer than 9 points, provide your phone number: _____

If You Can't Manage Them . . .

Preparation Rubric

Class Period, Date(s)

Name: _____

	Rarely or Never 0-2 pts	Sometimes 3-5 pts	Most of the time 6-9 pts	Always 10 pts
I arrive to class on time.				
I bring all necessary materials.				
I bring completed assignments and homework.				

_____ points (of 30 pts)

If fewer than 20 points, provide your phone number: _____

Name _____

Class Period, Date(s) _____

RUBRIC FOR GETTING ALONG WITH OTHERS

Score	Description
1	I do not get along well with my peers. I tend to be argumentative or defensive. Frequently I refuse to follow classroom procedures and directions. I am often disruptive, display anger, or am involved in conflict.
2	I sometimes do not get along well with my peers. Sometimes I get argumentative or defensive. I sometimes refuse to follow directions or cooperate. Sometimes I am loud. Sometimes I am angry or disruptive.
3	I get along with others in general. I do not get involved in conflict. I follow directions and try my best not to be disruptive.
4	I get along very well with others in the classroom. I am flexible and agreeable. I don't ever disrupt. I follow directions well.

_____ points (of 4 pts)

If less than 3 points, provide your phone number: _____

Chapter 8

Direct, Clear Talk

Tell it like it is!

Straight Talk

Read each example of a vague teacher-to-student message. Write the message in straight talk—telling the student precisely what needs to happen or what he or she needs to do.

✔"Let's all calm down now."

✔"Darla, your behavior is unacceptable."

✔"Get rid of the things that distract from your work."

✔"I'm waiting for you to be ready."

✔"Get control of yourself, Will!"

✔"Judah, it's time for you to be more responsible."

✔"Simone, you do not look prepared."

✔"Jessica, that is not the way we sharpen pencils."

✔"Stop behaving like children."

The teacher had ten years of teaching experience—and had earned tenure. As a part of my Master Teacher responsibilities, I was asked to observe him and assess his proficiency in the classroom. (A possible bonus was in store if this teacher was deemed proficient!) Only a few minutes into the 30-minute observation, it was clear: This teacher needed some help with classroom management.

Now here's what was fascinating: His lesson was engaging. He was organized and ready to go. He knew his content. And he clearly had plenty of experience. But from the moment he started the lesson, his main form of gaining students' attention was to say, "Shhhhh." As a matter of fact, by the time my 30-minute observation was over, he had used "Shhhhh" 35 times. As I sat there in a class full of middle school students, I kept wondering how long it would be before some student shouted out "it" after one of the teacher's long "Shhhhh" reminders!

For those of you who haven't figured out where I am going with this story . . . . Well, since he tried it 35 times and it didn't work, this technique was clearly not effective. But more than that—"Shhhhh" should never be a part of your vocabulary when working with middle school or high school students.

"Wow, what an experience!" That's what I have to say about the honor it has been to visit the classrooms of tenured teachers and, at the same time, to mentor new teachers in our district. I've had the privilege of seeing teachers with 25 years of experience in action and those who are just beginning their fabulous careers in education. This has allowed me to watch, ask questions, discuss, brainstorm, and dialogue with a wide range of professionals about the real stuff of running a classroom.

If You Can't Manage Them . . .

Every Teacher Can Do This!

From these experiences (and those in my own classroom), I am certain that one simple management technique is an absolute must in every classroom. Any teacher can and should add this to a management toolbox: **Be direct!**

Here's what this means:

One

Be very precise about what you expect of students. Do not expect that they will automatically remember and follow the details of all rules and procedures. Spell it out. Say exactly what they are to do. Do this over and over.

> The more direct you are, using specifics, the more clearly students understand what is expected.

Two

Do not use subtleties or inferences about what you need them to do. Do not use generalities. The more direct you are, using specifics, the more clearly students understand what is expected.

Three

Be concise. Don't give long explanations, start a discussion, get into negotiations, or leave openings for arguments. Straight talk is about making a statement. When you are directing students about behavior—this is not the time to explain the thinking behind the rule (unless it is early in the year). You've explained the reasons for the rules and procedures long ago. This is a time for one thing—to say, plainly, what must happen now.

Four **Along with the straight talk, give choices.** Name the student, state clearly the behavior they are doing. Give a choice to stop, or give a choice of the consequence. (Middle school students, in particular, love choices. They'll respond to this!)

Some teachers shy away from being direct. They tell me, "That's not who I am as a person." Understand that **direct** does not imply that you are **mean** or **confrontational**. This technique has nothing to do with your personality. I have seen quiet, laid-back middle or high school teachers be extremely direct without ever raising their voices. (In fact, soft-spoken teachers often use this with exceptional effectiveness.) Being direct simply means you are telling the student exactly what you need them to do. This method of redirection is referred to as using "I need" statements or other statements that describe exact behaviors.

TERRY, YOU MAY TAKE THE SNAKE BACK TO THE SCIENCE LAB NOW OR SPEND LUNCH PERIOD FOR THE REST OF YOUR LIFE WITH PRINCIPAL CRANK. WHICH DO YOU CHOOSE?

To Be or Not To Be (Direct)

It is easy to miss opportunities to be direct. Many of us are so used to using vague reminders or instructions. OR we easily slide into discussions, negotiations, or long explanations—when all it takes is a simple statement of what needs to happen NOW!

If You Can't Manage Them . . .

Direct Talk? NO!

Go back and review the teacher reflection on page 182. Read the examples and your ideas for straight talk. Here are some further examples of nonspecific questions and requests from the teacher. Combine this list with that on the "Straight Talk" exercise to get a good look at what NON-direct talk looks like:

- "Your homework attitude needs an adjustment."
- "Now class, remember to follow the rules."
- "You are being disrespectful."
- "Andrew, you know what you should be doing. Do it."
- "Get with the program, Shaun!"
- "Have you taken something from Anya?"
- "Be ready to listen."
- "Shhhhhhhhhh! Shhhhhhhhhh! Shhhhhhhhhhh!"
- "Class! Class! Class!"
- "Luke, what is it you think you are doing?"
- "Ramon, your class participation is not acceptable."
- "This is not the way we behave during class discussions."
- "Whoever is talking— it needs to stop now."
- "I'm waiting!"

CLASS, ANYONE WHO IS BEHAVING INAPPROPRIATELY, PLEASE THINK ABOUT WHAT YOU ARE DOING.

Direct Talk? Yes!

Here are some alternatives—direct ones!

- "Lucas, you are waving your arms and shouting. I need you to control your body, stop speaking, and take your seat."

- "Karla, you have not turned in homework for six days. I need it all tomorrow morning before class begins."

- "Julie, your notes from friends, your cell phone, your iPod, and your makeup kit are interfering with your work. I need you to start putting all of these in your backpack immediately."

- "Judah, being a responsible student means completing all your assignments. You can stop talking and finish this project now. Or you may join me here after school until it is done. Which do you choose?"

- "Tomas, Lucy, Brett, Gabby, and Tad—talking out of turn is not okay in this class. Notice Rule #3 on the wall. I expect all of you to stop this behavior, starting now."

- "Sadie, you pushed over Emma's backpack and scattered her belongings all over. You are disrespecting her and her stuff. I need you to go back over there, apologize to Emma, and carefully return her things to her backpack. I expect to see no facial expressions or gestures of disrespect as you do this."

- "Jessica, the rule is that pencils are sharpened at the beginning of class, and in a quiet manner that does not disrupt. The time is wrong, and you are loud and disruptive. Return to your seat now."

- "Les and Miguel, potty jokes are not befitting of eighth graders or appropriate for school. Stop them now."

If You Can't Manage Them . . .

- "Darla, that gesture was rude and disrespectful. It does not belong in school—ever. This is what will happen now: You will take your things and wait for me in the hall."

- "To every one of you in the back row (give names)—It is time for your books to be open, your pencils to be in your hands, and your eyes to be on me. This is what it means to be prepared."

- "Shaun, I need you to stand up, walk forward, and hand me the cell phone."

- "Leanne, Anya's cell phone is in your back pocket. It belongs in Anya's hand. I expect to see it in Anya's hand within one second."

- "Will, it is time for you to get off the table and stand quietly by my desk with your arms and legs perfectly still."

- "Simone, I see that you have no pencil, paper, homework, or book out. This shows me that you are not prepared. Can you get prepared by the time I walk over to your desk, or do we need a discussion at lunchtime?"

- "Class, it is time to listen. This means your desk is clear, you are facing me, your hands are folded on top of your desk, and your mouth is closed."

- "I expect to hear no voices other than mine for the next three minutes."

- "Luke, your hand is in Todd's desk. Put both of your hands on top of your desk."

- "Ramon, the appropriate way to participate is to wait your turn. Can you stop blurting out, or would you like to stay in during break for some rehearsal of appropriate behavior?"

- "Andrew, now is the time for you to get out of the wastebasket and into your seat."

- "Sophie, Katy, Carla, and Paul, your talking is disruptive. Your chatter needs to stop now."

- "I expect all of you to have your finished assignment on your desk in thirty seconds."

In an out-of-control classroom, the teacher stands around waiting for students to quiet down. This could take a long time— maybe forever.
– Joe, grade 8

Scenarios and Advice

Here are some actual situations from my classroom, along with some good advice I have found or been given:

- John had decided that during every transition he would touch, push, or make faces at anyone with whom he came into contact. (Oh, the joys of teaching the hormonally challenged middle schooler!) Being direct with John sounded like this: "John, I need you to stop pushing, touching, and making faces. John, you have two choices: one— you can stop, or two—you can stay after the bell rings. What would you like to do?"

- Doug Lemov, author of *Teach Like a Champion* (2010), says that many a student comes to the classroom not necessarily wanting to be disrespectful, but simply not knowing how to be a student. I had to realize that students may blurt out or interrupt because that is what they do at home, and so they

If You Can't Manage Them . . .

think it is okay to do it in class—not because they intend to be rude to me.

Lemov goes on to say that part of the responsibility of the teacher is to teach students what it looks like to be a student. As a teacher, you need to continually remind students what is expected of them as students in your classroom. Of course, being direct and specific is one great way to do this. This helps to minimize problematic behavior, but it also teaches them how to be students. Use language such as . . .

all eyes on me

pencils down, mouths closed

knees facing the front of the room

keep your eyes on me and now follow me to the board

this is what it looks like to be a student

• • • • I vividly remember Tyler (a walking litterbug), his pencils and papers falling out of his bag, his shirt disheveled, his shoes untied. The bell would ring; everyone would be in a seat—but not Tyler. He didn't even realize the bell had rung. I decided to use Doug Lemov's advice and help teach Tyler how to be a student.

So here's how it went: The bell would ring and I would say, "Tyler, you need to be in your seat. Students are seated when the bell rings. Tyler, eyes on me, nice job . . . now that's being a student."

I made it a point to end every redirection with Tyler by saying, "That's being a student," so Tyler would know exactly what students were supposed to do. I tried to be direct and precise in working with Tyler, hoping that he would eventually know what it meant to be a student in my class.

Let's just say it was a year-long project with ups and downs. But I did manage to get Tyler in his seat when the bell rang without having to tell him each day. (Baby steps, people, baby steps!)

• • • • Another way to look at being direct is to consider the "Warm Demander" model. This term, coined by researcher Judith Kleinfeld (1975), describes a teacher who treats students with unconditional positive regard and belief in the student's ability to succeed. Kleinfeld combines this with a teaching style she called "active demandingness." By this, she means a teacher who holds students to high standards.

> A good manager is very direct and has a strong voice. She or he expects that everybody will behave well.
>
> – Graham, grade 9

Much has been written about warm demander pedagogy. You probably know some of these teachers. In my experience, they speak firmly and with a matter-of-fact tone. They are brilliant at avoiding power struggles. They speak directly when faced with a situation that is not productive for the class. Warm demanders refuse to take no for an answer and have high behavior expectations for all their students. They love their students so much that they are willing to demand excellence from each of them.

If You Can't Manage Them . . .

> Students accept your directness— because they know you care about them enough to push them.

• • • • Writing about directness, I am reminded of a former student, Natalie—the loudest seventh grade girl who ever walked through my classroom door. She could never speak in a normal tone; rather, she felt the need to yell whatever she had to say. Natalie was so loud that I had the nurse do a hearing test with her because I was certain she had to be partly deaf. There was no deafness—just her need to be heard by me and everyone else in hallway 600. Once I knew that her hearing was fine, I knew I had to address the issue before I went insane and lost my own hearing.

So, the next time Natalie announced her arrival and proceeded to interject at a level that was clearly inappropriate, I said, "Natalie, I need you to bring the volume of your voice down when you walk into my room, when you answer questions, and when you work in groups. I know you can do it, and I expect to see this starting tomorrow when you come to class."

That's all it took. Natalie arrived the next day, I reminded her as she entered the room, and a new Natalie emerged—one that was much more pleasant to be around. At the end of the day I made sure to thank her and tell her how proud I was of her for choosing to lower her voice. Being direct and specific with Natalie, was all she needed to change her behavior. I had a very strong relationship with Natalie so I knew I could be very direct with her and she would respond. For Natalie, it was also very important that I acknowledged and praised her on the days she was a superstar.

• • • • • • • • •

Being direct with students is a valuable skill for classroom management. But teachers must first establish a deep, caring relationship with each student— only then is directness effective. In the context of strong, positive teacher–student relationships, students accept your directness—because they know you care about them enough to push them.

Straight-Talk Directions

We've all been there or will be there—standing in front of our class, giving instructions as to what we want students to do. And as soon as we say, "Get started," several students give that confused look and ask, "What are we supposed to do?"

Oh, the joys of working with adolescents! After teaching for the past 18 years, I have started to reconsider how I give instructions. (Yes, I guess this means I am a slow learner!) I want to eliminate the frustration I feel and the frustration I know some of my students feel when I have to repeat myself. We teachers are so troubled when our students can't follow directions. But if we don't train them in this skill, why do we complain?

Gain some freedom from the dreaded cry, "But what are we supposed to do?"

If You Can't Manage Them . . .

Learning to talk straight to students extends beyond the realm of monitoring and teaching appropriate behavior. To be successful students, they need to learn to listen carefully and follow directions. But they can't learn this skill if we give muddled, complex, unthoughtful directions. This may seem like a small thing, but it helps with classroom management! It is extremely frustrating (and time-wasting) to spend several minutes explaining something only to find they weren't paying attention in the first place. Try some of these suggestions about instruction-giving. They should help you get some freedom from the dreaded cry, "But what are we supposed to do?" They just might help reduce your stress and contribute to our students' satisfaction and productivity.

BUT I GAVE REAL CLEAR DIRECTIONS FOR MAKING AN OCTAHEDRON.

OOPS!

1. Stop! Think and Reflect!

Anticipate the challenges your activity may pose, both with the activity itself, and with explaining the directions. Write it out ahead of time. Share this with a colleague to see if it is clear.

2. Be straight, short, and simple.

Keep verbal instructions short and simple—no longer than one minute. You will get students' attention for only one minute, so break longer instructions into smaller chunks. For example, I can give the first part of the instructions and have students pair and share what they just heard. Students then return their attention to me, I do a quick review, and then I add the next set of instructions.

3. Write a list.

Show a written list of instructions on a screen, active board, or other board. Or give a checklist to each student or group. Students can follow along with your directions and check off

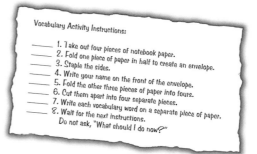

Vocabulary Activity Instructions:

——— 1. Take out four pieces of notebook paper.
——— 2. Fold one piece of paper in half to create an envelope.
——— 3. Staple the sides.
——— 4. Write your name on the front of the envelope.
——— 5. Fold the other three pieces of paper into fours.
——— 6. Cut them apart into four separate pieces.
——— 7. Write each vocabulary word on a separate piece of paper.
——— 8. Wait for the next instructions.
    Do not ask, "What should I do now?"

each step after they are sure they understand it. Walk around to see that they are indeed doing this. Then this becomes an aid for them to use as they work. When you create board games, glue or write the rules and directions on the back of the board.

4. Create a visual aid.

Hold up or post a diagram. Show students a finished example. Project visual models to show steps. Give students a picture of completed examples.

5. Give time for questions.

Offer students an opportunity to ask any questions about the task they are to complete. Once you feel that all questions have been answered, end the discussion time.

6. Lose your voice!

Once students have heard instructions, seen them in writing, and asked questions—it is time to set them free. Tell students they must follow the directions WITHOUT asking you any further questions. They can certainly ask their group members or neighbors if necessary. However,

If You Can't Manage Them . . .

if they ask you, they will lose several points on the assignment. You might be surprised at how many students do the assignment on their own and do it well.

Don't hesitate to be specific and direct when working with students. When you use direct talk with students, you help them understand what acceptable behavior is, you help to further their experiences with self-control, and you teach them how to be successful students. When you give straightforward, simple directions—you help students catch on fast to tasks and successfully complete learning activities. These accomplishments help students feel like superstars (especially when you tell them they are)! The part of the adolescent brain (male brain in particular) that helps students make good decisions about behavior and be good students is still in need of a growth spurt. This is all the more reason to be vigilant—constantly reminding, redirecting, and talking straight to your students as they try to manage their own behavior.

Chapter 9

Gender Matters

Disciplining boys and girls IS different.

Pondering Differences

1. On plain paper, draw a large outline of a male figure.
2. On the head, write three things you believe you know about the adolescent male brain.
3. Near the heart, describe how boys process or express their feelings.
4. On the left leg, note two learning activities you use to allow boys to move.
5. On the right leg, write what you most enjoy about working with boys.
6. On the left arm, note a behavior issue you find is different for boys than for girls.
7. On the right arm, describe one difference you find between managing girls and boys.

1. On plain paper, draw a large outline of a female figure.
2. On the head, write three things you believe you know about the adolescent female brain.
3. Near the heart, note how you think girls process or express their feelings.
4. On the left leg, write two learning strategies you use for girls only.
5. On the right leg, write what you most enjoy about working with girls.
6. On the left arm, write two reasons you think there seems to be a lot of drama in girls' behavior.
7. On the right arm, write something you've noticed about managing girls.

Girls can make the Duracell® battery look weak. Yes, they can outlast the Energizer Bunny. Their mouths just do not stop! The bell can ring. I can be standing in front of the class directing students to their seats. And every time (I mean EVERY class period), there are two or three girls who cannot bear the thought of separating from one another. They cannot fathom putting their conversation on hold.

And then there's the male obsession with drumming. Particularly in recent years, I have noticed how many boys have the need to use their pencils and their desks (or textbooks, math tools, the globe, maps—anything) as personal drum sets. And they can't stop—any more than the girls can stop talking. I swear, I feel like I operate in the middle of a dysfunctional rock band!

It is impossible NOT to notice. In my classroom, over all my years of teaching, it just IS a reality that the behavior issues differ for girls and boys. Student response to discipline strategies and teacher reaction differ as well. Different tactics work with males than with females.

I don't want to set stereotypes here, and I don't want to diminish individual differences. I don't mean to say that ALL boys react the same and that ALL girls react the same—or that there are not many, many similarities between the sexes when it comes to management and behavior. But I have much more success with management since I recognized, learned about, and adjusted to the differences that my experience shows to be obvious.

If You Can't Manage Them . . .

Let's Face It!

Other teachers overwhelmingly confirm this. Whenever I work with teachers on classroom management, I ask, "So, which group do you think is more difficult to manage in a classroom— boys or girls?" Some say boys; others say girls. What we all agree on is that in many situations most girls and boys react, interact, and process differently. We also agree that we need help with seeing and responding to these differences.

It's impossible NOT to notice that discipline issues differ between boys and girls.

When I had the delightful opportunity to teach 25 boys and 4 girls in one class, I got a crash course in how different a classroom becomes when the majority of students are of one sex. Not only did I recognize the dissimilarity in behavior right away, but I also knew it was time to do some research on behavioral differences between boys and girls and begin to apply that information to my classroom management. I needed help—and fast!

One of the books that helped me most is *Why Gender Matters* by Dr. Leonard Sax. It's a must-read for anyone who works with kids! Dr. Sax shares research, strategies, and many ideas to provoke thought and self-examination. In this chapter, I want to share techniques and considerations about working with and managing the two sexes. These ideas mix insights from Dr. Sax with my own experiences and suggestions.

Managing Boys

I believe boys are at a disadvantage because many schools function in a manner that is easier for most girls than for most boys. Rules such as "sit in your seats," "listen to the teacher," "follow directions," and "raise your hand" are all behaviors that are generally tougher for boys to follow than for girls. Consider these ideas and suggestions as you think specifically about managing boys:

1. **Boys need to move.** If you work with preadolescents and adolescents, you know this without reading any research! As a middle school teacher, I would add this: They also need to push, shove, tackle, burp, and share other bodily functions on a regular basis. If boys do not get enough movement within a class, they will do one of two things: disengage and become inattentive OR become disruptive, fidget and squirm, or blurt out. In either case, you have a behavior problem. Believe me, if you don't plan for boys to move—they'll move anyway (but not according to your plan)!

   • Koosh® balls can help students who have the constant need to move and fidget. Instead of tearing up paper, tossing pencils, drumming on the desk, or punching his neighbor, a kid can squeeze a ball. This does help some students concentrate! (You are probably thinking, "What? You want me to give objects that could become flying missiles to already-antsy middle school boys? Are you nuts?")

I offer a Koosh® ball to everyone—with the rule that they cannot be projected in any way. If you explain clear expectations and follow through consistently, their use will actually reduce, rather than create, management problems. As the year progresses, I find that only a few students (mostly boys) continue to use them.

• • • • A science teacher colleague uses this idea: He has replaced all seats in his classroom with those big bouncy exercise balls. He says it's going great. Kids get a chance to use their bodies and get slight movement. (This builds muscle strength and control and improves posture—both of which contribute to better brain function.) On days when a student can't handle this or pushes the rules, he or she gets the chair back. My colleague says he is firm and consistent on this, and never takes balls away from the whole group for the actions of a few.

• • • • As I mentioned at the beginning of the chapter, many boys need to use their pencils and desks as drum sets. Trying to stop this became an everyday battle in my classroom. Finally, I went to the fabric store and bought several squares of foam core. I told students that I did not want to crush their dreams of becoming rock stars, but if they had to tap their pencils, they would

Believe me, if you don't plan for boys to move, they'll move anyway.

have to do so on the foam core—not on their desks. Once the students started drumming and realized no one could hear it (especially me), the need to jam out suddenly vanished.

It is imperative to find ways for boys to move. If you don't, boys will constantly remind you in ways you wish would go away.

2. **Boys do not hear as well as girls.** In *Why Gender Matters*, Dr. Sax reviews several studies on the hearing of newborn babies—the results of which indicate that girls clearly hear better than boys. Follow-up studies conclude that this difference continues through the teenage years (pgs 15–18). One study found that the average baby girl had an immediate brain response 80% greater than the response of the average baby boy (pg 17).

What does this mean for you? Realize that some misbehavior or "not listening" could simply be the result of the boys not hearing instructions well. If the teacher's voice is female, the higher tone may be even harder for boys to hear. So have boys sit closer to the front of the room. Or circulate near them. If a boy seems to be having particular trouble attending, make sure you are near him when you give instructions. Project your voice well. Use an amplifier if necessary.

3. **Boys respond very well to directness.** When I coached the seventh grade boys' basketball team, I quickly learned how effective it is to simply be direct. When I told boys specifically what to do, I got much faster and better results with their behavior than when

I suggested, implied, asked for cooperation, or asked questions. Dr. Sax says it this way: "When you work with boys, don't ask; tell" (pg 173).

Ask any student if he or she wants to stop doing something, and you have given them an option to say no. A boy may feel especially challenged and thus obligated to take the "no" option. Not long ago, I watched a young teacher discipline a child in the hallway. She told him exactly what to do, but ended the conversation with "All right?" That one question gave the young man options to comply or not (and he chose not to). TELL boys exactly what you want them to do or stop doing. Remember: Be direct, specific, and avoid using "okay?" or "all right?" at the end of your conversation.

> **Tell boys exactly what you want them to do or stop doing.**

Here's an example:

- **Not Direct:** "Elijah, would you refrain from bothering your classmates? Okay?"

- **Direct:** "Elijah. Stop punching Nick. Come here immediately and stand beside me."

4. **Do not confront boys in front of their buddies.** This can lead to disaster. Boys will do everything in their power to show their pals that they are not intimidated—even by a teacher.

The teacher directed Josh to put a paper away before starting a project. He complied, but snuck it out again. He thought the teacher was not looking, but she was, and told him he was being disobedient and defiant. Even though this was true, the teacher incited embarrassment and anger by saying it in front of the class. Josh came back quickly with, "I don't even want this stupid paper!"

This escalated the problem. Josh ended up in the hall, which cost him time away from the lesson but allowed him to show his friends that he was not afraid of the teacher. This could have been a nonissue if the teacher had spoken quietly to Josh out of hearing of the class.

5. **Ask boys what they think, not how they feel.** In *Why Gender Matters*, Dr. Sax shows how differences in development of male and female brains (particularly in the parts where emotions occur and where talking originates) lead to differences in ability to express feelings (pgs 29–30). The faster development of these parts in females enables girls to tell you how they feel (even when you don't want to know). For boys, the development and connections occur later (if at all, some women would argue), making it difficult for boys to understand or describe how they are feeling.

   The next time you have a discussion with a boy about a behavioral incident, ask him what he thinks rather than how he feels. You might be surprised to actually hear more than, "I don't know."

6. **Boys are often reluctant to ask for help.** I am sure you have heard that old adage that a man would rather remain lost than ask for directions! I see this every day in my classroom, especially when boys are working on an assignment in groups with other boys. Here's what happens: Boys are suddenly misbehaving in their group. I wander over and find out that they are simply stuck and

don't know what to do next. I ask, "Well, why didn't you raise your hands and ask for help?" And, yes, I get the wonderful (expected) answer of "I don't know." (Perhaps the answer is that boys don't want to be seen as studious, eager to achieve, or needing help.)

WHAT ARE YOU FEELING?

I FEEL LIKE HITTING HIM!

Swing by the boys' groups often to check in. Prepare a written list of the steps or tasks that make up the assignment. Put this in a place that is visible to all groups as they work. This will cut out a lot of "lostness" and resulting misbehavior.

7. **If you are fair, most boys will "fess up" to the misbehavior and move on.** I find this to be one of the most refreshing aspects of working with boys. With boys, I can name the behavior, issue the consequence, and go on with my day. (Girls? Well, I'll talk about that later!) The operative phrase here is "If you are fair." The quick recovery from an incident happens ONLY if boys think you are fair (treating all students the same) in your redirection and consequences.

Isaac was a very smart, rambunctious seventh grader who loved to talk, even when I was talking (or when anyone else was talking, for that matter). After twice redirecting Isaac on this problem, I sent him into the hall so I could compose myself and, I hope, put an end to this behavior. In the hall, I asked Isaac, "Why do you think I sent you out here?" He answered that it was because of his talking, but added that he thought that I redirected only him—not Johnny or Billy—for talking. Basically he told me that from his perspective I was not being fair.

Isaac emphatically rejected my offer to talk to Johnny and Billy about the conversation. (I find this a common response from boys.) I did promise to observe them more closely and redirect them when they were talking. This seemed to pacify Isaac, who settled down and stopped his constant chatter. I kept my promise to Isaac, noting when the other two boys needed redirection. Remember—you must follow through on your promises to students. Otherwise they will lose faith in you and your word.

8. **Boys need a safe place and method to express their angst and aggression.** It is no wonder that contact sports are so popular with boys. It is the one place where they can hit, push, shove, tackle, run, and not get into trouble. It is a must to find appropriate ways for boys to release their aggression. This is in the best interest of everyone involved. Mostly, it is in the best interest of the boy himself. You can include movement appropriately within classroom learning activities.

However, sometimes a boy cannot control himself all day, and you may have to take other steps to address this need. Here's an example: Jared was a troubled boy. His mom was in prison for selling drugs. Dad was in and out of rehabilitation. And his family was constantly one step from being homeless. Jared was angry and extremely moody. If he was in a bad mood, look out! He refused to

If You Can't Manage Them . . .

work, was bossy, pouted, and shouted, "I don't care" a thousand times throughout the class time.

Because I worked hard to build a relationship with Jared, his behavior in my class was mild compared to other classes. Still, it was tough. I knew he was suffering in ways most other students could not imagine; yet I could not let Jared get away with those behaviors. I made an arrangement to give Jared a reasonable way to work out his aggression. When he was feeling too angry, upset, or simply too crabby to handle class, I would allow him to go with one of our hall paraprofessionals to the gym to use the punching bag.

FIVE MINUTES AGO,
CAM AND DAMIEN WERE
IN A KNOCKDOWN,
DRAG-OUT ALTERCATION.

Now, this strategy was possible, first, because I had a strong relationship with Jared. I thought I could trust that he was being honest with me in his need to release his aggression. Second, this was accompanied by strict guidelines. He could be gone only 10 minutes; he had to return on time; and when he returned, he had to participate appropriately, not complain, and be the model student I knew he could be. He knew that if these guidelines were not followed, he would not be allowed to go the next time. I had to hold tightly to these expectations and follow through when they were not met.

With such a strategy, students might ask why Jared gets this "privilege." I handle this by quoting the title from Rick Wormeli's book, *Fair Isn't Always Equal* (2006).

I ask students to tell me what this quote means to them and for our classroom. When discussing a specific situation like Jared's, I am careful not to divulge to the students why Jared needs to leave the room. I only say something like this: "I know this may seem unfair to some of you, but you need to trust me on this one."

9. **Most boys LOVE competition.** Boys thrive on the team concept, the challenge of victory or defeat. To help engage and manage boys, implement some competitive activities and look for ways to encourage teamwork. I often create review games with a competitive element. For example, they can shoot a Nerf® ball into a basket (my trash can) if their team answers a question correctly. Or, if they land on a particular square in a board game, they get to do jumping jacks.

   Here's one way I remind them about teamwork: In every one of our class share times (this never fails!), some boy will offer something like this: "I won my hockey (or baseball or soccer or so on) game last night" or "I won my baseball game yesterday." Every time, I respond by saying, "You won that game all by yourself?" They always look at me with a puzzled look until they understand that they need to use "we" instead of "I" when sharing about their latest team victories.

10. **Got boys? You've got posturing!** Boys want other students to know who they are or what they are like. This can manifest itself in blurting, laughing at inappropriate times, or simply making inappropriate comments—things that turn into disruptions and

problems. So, on the first day of school, I talk to each class about posturing. I tell boys that they certainly CAN posture, but that if I deem it inappropriate or if it breaks classroom rules, there will be consequences. Trust me, the posturing does not go away simply because I talk about it. But addressing it up front defuses some of the effects. And, when it happens inappropriately, I am prepared to address the behavior with consequences.

> A good manager holds the same expectations for all students, but disciplines them as individuals.
>
> – Marie, middle school parent

Managing Girls

The dynamics of girls' behaviors have changed over the years of my teaching. I find that there is more physical fighting at school among girls, that they are more outwardly verbal in class, and that they are much more willing to challenge authority. Here are some thoughts and strategies I have found helpful when managing girls:

1. **Girls can use nonverbals with deadly force.** I have been annihilated several times by girls giving me the "look to kill." The eye rolling, the huffing sound, and the flip of the hair are all techniques girls have mastered to perfection to show their disdain for you or for your requests or expectations. These signals are freely used on classmates, as well.

Do this the first day of school: Demonstrate the nonverbal behaviors you deem disrespectful, especially for your girls. I roll my eyes, make the huffing sound, and try to flip my hair to make sure my girls, in particular, clearly understand that disrespectful nonverbals are not allowed in our classroom. As I mimic these behaviors, the class gets a great chuckle. But they also get the point. After that, when a girl uses one of these tactics, I specifically name the behavior she demonstrated and remind her that what she did was disrespectful.

By the way, girls read nonverbal signals as well as they dish them out. So be sure to keep your own nonverbals in check. You may be thinking you'd like to toss a girl out the window, but you had better not let her figure that out. Girls are keen at observing what is around them and sensing the pleasure or displeasure in messages from the person with whom they are engaged. When you want a girl to know you approve of her, look her directly in the eye and smile (Sax, 2005).

2. **Girls can talk, talk, talk, and talk.** When you have to discipline girls, it is helpful to understand their brain development. The brain connections that lead to great verbal ability for many girls, we could say, are "locked and loaded." These areas develop more quickly in females (Sax, pgs 29–30).

> I've been annihilated several times by a girl giving me the "look to kill."

I always start a discipline conversation with girls by asking the following question: "Would you like to go first and describe what has happened, or should I?"

Ninety-nine percent of the time, the girl will want to go first. I mean, come on, girls have a lot to say! I find that it's helpful to let a girl talk until she gets everything off her chest that she needs to express.

Because girls are so verbal, they interrupt you if they feel what you are saying is not valid. Many times I have to say to the young lady, "Okay, please do not interrupt me. I listened to you; now I expect you to listen to me. You'll get another chance to talk when I am finished."

3. **When disciplining girls, STICK to your message.** Before you plan to discuss the situation with the girl, know exactly what you are going to say and do not deviate from that message.

   Here's an example: I had a female eighth grade student who conducted side conversations during class on a regular basis. Because I was so frustrated, I had not properly prepared my message before our discussion. You would think it would be simple to say, "Stop the side conversations," but instead I said, "You are talking all the time and never seem to stop."

   She responded by attacking one word—"never." I still hear her today: "I don't never stop talking, never means I never stop. That is not true. I do stop talking. I'm not talking all the time . . . ." She went on and on, staying with this tone.

   Instead of accusing and generalizing, I needed to be specific, direct—staying on message with something like this: "A few minutes ago, you were having a side conversation with Julie. I need you to stop having side conversations while I am talking." (I also needed to just keep repeating that statement.)

Never get into a word match with a middle or high school girl. She will tear you up and spit you out before you know what has hit you. Instead, remember to prepare your message before you engage her, give her a choice to talk first, let her talk, and stick to your message.

4. **Often girls perceive that you are yelling at them.** The research about hearing discrepancies between boys and girls suggests that noise levels that distract girls can be ten times softer than levels that distract boys (Elliott, 1971). If you are a male teacher, be aware that a girl may perceive your voice as yelling. If you are a female teacher, be aware that when you speak louder than usual in frustration, anger, or urgency—girls may interpret the communication as yelling. The result may be anger or defensiveness. In addition, the female brain development that leads to emotional acuity can cause a girl to pick up the slightest displeasure or distress and interpret it as yelling.

> Never get into a word match with a middle or high school girl.

5. **Girls can relate to and give "I feel" statements.** As mentioned earlier, female brain development makes it possible for girls to be more in tune with emotions (Sax, pgs 29–30). They can talk about how they feel in a certain situation. Through a mental skill called "induction," a girl can imagine herself in the position of the other person in a

If You Can't Manage Them . . .

situation (Sax, pg 181.) More so than boys, girls are able to answer the question, "How would you feel if this happened to you?" This means that it does work to talk to girls about the feelings of all parties in a conflict.

6. **Be direct with girls—but do it differently.** If you could watch me in action, you would see a different variety of directness for girls than for boys—something I call "conversational directness." I find that girls do not respond well to a very firm tone. When I make a direct request such as, "Sit down, NOW" in a tone of voice that does *not* convey compassion, there may be a negative response. Many girls will feel this as bossiness or anger, and will react by being defensive, verbally aggressive, and dismissive.

BUT MR. LEE, I CAN'T GIVE UP MY CELL PHONE! I'LL *DIE* WITHOUT IT. WAHHHH!

Conversational directness delivers the same direct message, but uses a calmer tone. For example, you might say, "Hey, Maria, I need you to sit down. Thanks." You are still telling Maria exactly what to do, but you are using a tone to which most girls will respond positively.

7. **Most girls want the approval of the teacher.** Most girls have a great desire to please the teacher and want to connect with the teacher on a personal level. Earlier in the book, I told you about how every year some students ask me if they can call me Kim. Only girls have asked me this question. Girls need you to acknowledge that they are doing a good job, that you approve of their work, and that you accept them for who they are. It is vital

for teachers, especially male teachers, to recognize that many middle and high school girls lack self-esteem. Work to show acceptance with simple actions such as smiling, nodding your head, or giving a girl a high-five. This will work wonders for improving their comfort and their behavior!

8. **Most girls love group work and are very effective and productive within those groups.** Because of girls' highly developed verbal skills (not to mention their insatiable need for social interaction), it is only logical that they should work in groups. Girls can do some amazing research, problem solving, and thinking within group assignments. Group work gives them solid experiences in listening to each other (something they NEED), and working together with respect and fairness.

However, if the group of girls falls apart, it can be pretty nasty, and is usually difficult to salvage. Things were going smoothly with a group of girl students working on a final project—until two girls decided they didn't like the third girl. I tried everything to rectify the situation so they could save their project and their grade. It became so ugly that parents were calling me saying that they would not allow their daughters to go to each other's houses to work on the assignment. To avoid the next World War in my classroom, I had to disband the group. Here's the lesson I learned: DO have clear expectations for group behavior and work. Don't let a group get to the point of irreparable conflict.

If You Can't Manage Them . . .

9. **Girls get mad and stay mad—sometimes forever.**
   Preadolescent and adolescent girls have the ability to remember everything a friend, teacher, or parent has done or not done. They can remember dates, times, actions, and precise quotes to support a position against someone considered an adversary.

I'll never forget a particular seventh grade girl who was super mad at me. Cautiously, I asked her how long she planned to be mad at me. She looked up and said, "Forever!" I was cracking up on the inside because I knew there was no way this girl could stay mad at me all year. She did, however, stay mad for a few days.

When a girl is mad, I encourage you to first (and foremost) validate her right to be angry in the first place. Then be clear to distinguish between the feeling itself and the inappropriate behavior that may flow from it. I tell all my students, "Your anger is okay. Disrespectful or harmful behavior is not okay."

When a girl has stopped being mad and can move on, it is important to affirm her. For example, I may say, "Hey, Kay, I am so proud of you for not allowing your anger to get in the way of the great day you are about to have. I can only imagine how difficult it was for you to get over it, but I am impressed with your willingness to let this go and move on with your day."

It's a big deal for girls to get past being angry. From my experience, I find that with good modeling and encouragement, girls can change the pattern.

10. **Got girls? You've got drama!** Ben Franklin missed something with his adage, "There are only two things that are certain in life: death and taxes." He could have added, ". . . and, where there are girls—drama." Girl drama is alive and well in most middle and high schools. Drama can be inspired by and intensify over something as innocent as one girl not saying hello to another girl in the hallway.

Both boys and girls display aggression, but girls are more likely to be involved in behaviors such as rumors, gossip, and social exclusion. This is called *relational aggression*, which is behavior that is intended to hurt someone by harming his or her relationships with others (Crick & Grotpeter, 1995). Girls will ask their friends to ignore the girl they are mad at, encourage their friends to spread rumors about this individual, and basically inflict harm on the girl by excluding her from the social group.

THIS IS A DISASTER! I ONLY GOT AN **A MINUS** ON MY REPORT!

OH NO!

THE THIRD PERIOD DRAMA QUEENS ARE AT IT AGAIN.

Social media, such as Facebook™, emailing, instant messages, and texting, have added another layer to the girl drama. How many girl fights at school have started over the weekend on Facebook™ or Twitter®? How many times are girls mad at each other because one is spreading a rumor about the other by text or on a social network? You can bet that what happens one evening on social networks will flow into your classroom the next day.

If You Can't Manage Them . . .

It is simply impossible for a teacher to ignore the drama; it disrupts the flow and routine of your classroom. But, there are things you can do to decrease the tension, angst, and drama from disrupting your class. First, build strong relationships with your students. Second, be firm and consistent in responding to the drama. Then, girls will know that drama cannot enter your classroom without your addressing it.

Regularly, some girl will tell me she does not want to work with "so and so" today because she does not like her any more. (I know these girls will probably be best friends again tomorrow.) Because girls see their teachers as their allies, it is important to handle such situations in a firm, but loving way. I usually respond with, "Wow, I'm sorry that is happening between the two of you because both of you are such great kids and good friends. So, for today I will make sure you don't have to work with her, but after today there are no guarantees I can or will continue this. It's not that I'm trying to be mean, but your first priority is to be a student in this class, and that means we work as a team, even with those teammates we don't necessarily like."

What I have done here is acknowledged that she is fighting, connected with her feelings, spoken in a conversational voice, and yet placed clear boundaries on what I expect the following day. Now if she arrives the next day and refuses to cooperatively work with anyone, including her ex-friend, then our conversation may move to the hall, or she will work by herself for all partner activities that day.

You can't avoid the girl drama when working with this age group. So be diligent and compassionate, but firm, and put a sign up on your door that says, "Drama stops here!"

Chapter 10

Culture Matters

Cultural and ethnic differences DO affect management.

THINGS THE TEACHER OUGHT TO KNOW ABOUT US!

MS. C GETS SOME MUCH-NEEDED LESSONS.

The Real Story

✔

1. Do you feel the same expectations, trust, hope, connections to, and belief in all students—regardless of their ethnicity?

2. Have you felt uncomfortable with students of an ethnicity other than your own? In what situations?

3. How does a student's ethnicity affect your discipline style (disciplining reluctantly, avoiding discipline, responding more or less quickly, responding more or less harshly, overlooking behavior, or not overlooking behavior)?

4. How does the ethnicity of parents affect the nature of your interactions with them?

Where I have referred to "black students" or "white students," please substitute phrases relevant to you, such as "students of ethnicity different from mine."

If You Can't Manage Them . . .

In 2007, I started an after-school program, Students On Academic Rise (SOAR), to address a definite achievement gap in my middle school. Fellow teachers believed that many of their students had academic ability but were far behind in the background skills and knowledge they needed for academic success. I devised a plan, solicited grant funds, and basically extended the school day for this identified group of students. My goal was to give these students the chance to gain the extra skills necessary to navigate the system and become equal students in our school. The students in SOAR are 99% African American and 1% Latino and white. I have learned more from these students than from any book about how to effectively work with students of different ethnicities or how to close the achievement gap.

Here I was, a white girl, in charge of a program to work with mostly black kids. What did I know? All I had were my teaching skills, my belief that all kids can learn, a track record of successful relationships with students, my sense of humor, and my willingness to battle any obstacles to give kids a chance. Yes, I'd had a bunch of training in equity learning, in closing the achievement gap, and in working with students of ethnic minorities. But when the real kids walked through the door, it took about five minutes to know that the training could not prepare me for teaching and loving them or trusting and being trusted by them.

If You Can't Manage Them . . .

New Management Challenges

The experiences in this SOAR program, coupled with the realities of teaching a new mix of students, are the best things that have ever happened to me as a teacher. I have stretched and grown, faced my biases and fears, examined my teaching strategies and beliefs, and had great challenges along with rich relationships.

Working with students of a different ethnicity brought me new management adventures. The language and tactics that had worked before were not always right for these new students. There were patterns of behavior, ethics, and beliefs unfamiliar to me. Thank goodness for the patience, honesty, and wisdom of my students! They have taught me many lessons I need to manage a classroom that works for ALL students.

I want to be clear that this chapter is about my personal experience. As I said, most of the students who entered the previously all-white school were black. The comments, ideas, and advice I offer here are not intended to explain a variety of different cultural or ethnic outlooks or to narrowly define the behaviors of any group of students. I sincerely wish to avoid stereotyping or overgeneralization. **Each student is an individual.** Each family is different. No one set of circumstances, behaviors, or patterns applies to all students of a particular ethnicity. I relate my experience because, as with sex differences, I cannot ignore this fact of my teaching life—that cultural differences DO affect management and discipline situations in the classroom.

I take the risk of tackling this topic here because of that fact. Many teachers **do** work with students whose ethnicities differ from the teacher's and perhaps from the majority of the other students in the school. I want to share my journey and encourage you to be open to the probability that you have something to learn from these students. I firmly believe that differences in communication, style, ideas, patterns, and cultural "rules" will affect your relationships with students of different ethnicity. I am sure that if you explore these differences, your classroom will be more comfortable and your students will learn and behave better!

The Fear Factor

> If we sense you are afraid of us, we will make your life miserable.
> – ShaDonte, grade 7

Each year, we take our SOAR students to the University of Minnesota where they become the experts on a panel before future school counselors. The graduate students have the opportunity to ask SOAR students questions about their lives as adolescents and as students—particularly as students of color in a predominantly white school.

On one visit the final question of the day was, "What is one piece of advice you would give teachers and counselors about working with students of color?"

I'll never forget the response. Without hesitation, seventh grader ShaDonte replied, "Don't be afraid of us. If we sense you are afraid of us, we will make your life miserable. Most of us really want for the teacher to be in charge."

I sat in the audience, struck by his answer (as were the rest of the adults). Instantly, I knew how powerful this was for us to hear and that it was important to hear more. (The university counseling class was all white

If You Can't Manage Them . . .

with the exception of one African American male.)
So I followed up by asking the panel of kids to give
specific ways they could tell if a teacher (or other staff
member) is afraid of black people.

They answered, *You can tell a teacher is afraid of us
when they*

- *see a group of us coming down the hall and
either go to the other side of the hallway or
turn around and go the other way.*

- *ignore a potentially negative situation with
a group of African American students rather
than confront the issue.*

- *allow us to act out, but redirect the white kids
when they do something wrong.*

- *kick us out of class for the same behaviors the
white kid just did seconds earlier. The white kid
gets a warning and we get sent to the office.*

In her book *Other People's Children* (1995), Lisa Delpit
tells readers:

*A twelve-year-old friend tells me that there
are three kinds of teachers in his middle
school: the black teachers, none of whom are
afraid of black kids; the white teachers, a few
of whom are not afraid of black kids; and the
largest group of white teachers, who are all
afraid of black kids. It is this last group that,
according to my young informant, consistently
has the most difficulty with teaching, and
whose students have the most difficulty with
learning (pgs 167–168).*

Which type of teacher are you?

- Are you a teacher who is comfortable in all situations with each of your students—no matter what their ethnicity?

- Are you hesitant to be direct, to challenge, or even to build a relationship with a student of different ethnicity?

- Do you react differently toward a group of African American males coming down the hallway than toward a group of white males?

- Do you move quickly to quiet a group of African American girls because their voices are loud? (Who determines what is considered loud, anyway?)

- Do you see sagging pants as a precursor to the kid being a thug and unmanageable in your classroom, especially if he is of a certain minority group?

- Are you hesitant or uncomfortable in your relationships with parents of different ethnicities?

My Best Advice

1. Get past the fear!

Meet this idea head-on. Answer the above questions and those on page 220 honestly. Don't be ashamed of your answers. Whatever our fears or biases are, we need to face and investigate them before we act on them.

If You Can't Manage Them . . .

Yes, it is difficult to teach, motivate, and love students who intimidate you or whom you fear. But notice that the young man said, "Most of us really want for the teacher to be in charge." If these kids watch you be direct, honest, and consistent—they will sense that you are in charge and will respond well. Instead of cooperating just because you are the teacher, they will respond because you respect them. By not being afraid of them and by being direct, you provide safety and show care.

2. Be direct—super direct!

In *Other People's Children,* Lisa Delpit emphasizes the need to be direct, particularly with African American students. According to her, when teachers (especially white teachers) are not direct, the students are confused as to what they are supposed to do. She tells about a principal whose white teachers were continually sending their black students to the office for disobeying the teacher. When the teacher would talk to the parents, the parents usually had this response: "They do what I say. If you just TELL them what to do, they will do it."

Recently, I presented Delpit's viewpoint in a classroom management workshop. I could see the African Americans in the audience nodding heads in agreement. At the break, a white teacher told me, "I almost lost my job once because I was not direct with my students. I thought if I would just be positive with the students and let them know I cared, all would be well."

She went on to tell me that a black colleague advised her, "You need to be direct, tell them exactly what you need them to do, and they will do it and respect you for it."

The teacher changed her method of redirection, and the behavior issues became minimal and manageable.

This has been my experience exactly. I see that many white middle class teachers communicate by "suggesting." When teachers "suggest," students interpret the message as giving them an option—not a directive. Don't suggest. Tell students exactly what to do. Then expect them to do it.

One final note here: Males, no matter the race, always seem to respond to directness. I have found, however, that if you are going to be direct with African American girls, it is best to first build a good trusting relationship. Otherwise, your directness may ignite fireworks!

3. Relationships! Relationships! They are a must!

Though I am adamant about the importance of building relationships with ALL students, I do notice that strong relationships with my students of another ethnicity are doubly powerful in breaching the trust gap. The students, then, are much more eager to learn and to behave well. I believe that many of these students see school as an extension of their family, with the teacher as the head of the household. So if you want to connect with these kids and inspire them academically, you must first build trusting relationships with them. You earn their trust by following through with what you say you will do. If you say you will check up on an assignment, then you'd better do so. If you promise to go to their game, you'd better show up.

If You Can't Manage Them . . .

Mack T. Hines III, author of *Black Kids & Classroom Management* (2010), has done extensive work in learning about teacher–student relationships. Hines interviewed a wide age range of students including Caucasian, Hispanic, and African American. He asked students the following question: "Is it important for you to have a relationship with your teacher to be successful in school?"

When teachers "suggest," students interpret the message as giving them an option—not a directive.

Most Caucasian students answered "no" to the question, making statements such as, "No, they are there to teach, not be my friend." Or, "No, teach the material and be done with it." African American students had a resounding "yes" to the question. They explained that relationship-building is important so teachers can understand them better, which in turn makes them more likely to want to learn from that individual teacher.

4. Get to know the parent(s) or guardian(s).

Create a positive relationship with Mom, Dad, or guardian. This is an important step in understanding their child, developing a partnership between family and school, and learning about their expectations for their child. To help develop a caring relationship with your students' families, it is important that your first call home should be a positive one. Ninety-three percent of African American parents report that their first call from the school is a negative one (Kunjufu, 2002).

If your first call cannot be a positive call, make sure you begin the conversation with something positive about their child. For example:

> *Hello, Ms. Johnson, this is Ms. Campbell from Hopkins West Junior High. Is this a good time to talk? (If they say no, ask when it would be a good time for them, and get a number where they can be reached.) I'm calling today to chat with you about Nick. Before we begin, I just want you to know that I love having Nick in class, and I enjoy his sense of humor. Do you see that side of Nick at home? Anyway, I just wanted to let you know that today Nick used some bad language in class, so I told him I'd give you a call and let you know. I'm sure it won't happen again, but I just wanted you to know. Do you, Ms. Johnson, have any questions? While I have you on the phone, I was wondering if you could help me understand Nick a little better as a student . . . how do you think he learns best? etc. You have been so helpful—thank you so much for visiting with me today. Have a great day.*

I have learned so much from my parents, not only about their children, but about how best to work with students of another ethnicity and their families. Here's one example: At the beginning of each SOAR year, we have a dessert bar where we invite the parents of the new families into school to learn about SOAR and meet the coaches. During the first two years, I would give a little speech, explain the program, and try to communicate our vision and goals for SOAR. These dessert bar meetings did not go as well as I had hoped. I could tell that the parents were leery of me, the program, and

If You Can't Manage Them . . .

THE TEACHER LISTENS
MORE THAN SHE TALKS.

maybe even the choice of desserts—who knew! I decided to call one of the parents and get some honest feedback.

I did get honest feedback! He said, "Kim, let us do the talking. Let the parents of the students who have been in SOAR tell the others what SOAR is about and why their child should be in it. Parents of color will listen to us. They're not listening to you because they do not trust you yet."

This was great advice! When you work with students of a different ethnicity, do not underestimate what you can learn from their parents. Just ask—and listen!

5. Realize that kids of color balance TWO worlds.

In her book *The Dreamkeepers: Successful Teachers of African American Children* (2009), Gloria Ladson-Billings found that African American parents thought teachers who did exceptionally well with their child had the following characteristics: enthusiasm, a consistent level of respect for parents, and the perception that teachers understood the need for students to operate in the dual worlds of their home community and the white community. As an educator, it is vital that you take the time to learn about the community from which your students of color come. What are the rules, traditions, and customs of their community and family?

Here's an example: Most white teachers or middle class teachers expect students to tell them when someone has done something wrong. Be aware that parents in some cultures, regardless of class, believe in "an eye for an eye." On the street, the code is retaliation, not "snitching" (Kunjufu, 2002). Once, two of our SOAR students were having an issue and threatening to "take each other out." One of their parents got wind that her daughter was being threatened and showed up at the class to find out what had happened. She told her daughter, in front of the other students, "If so and so puts a hand on you, you had better put your hands back on her. If not, you're going to get it worse at home."

I was dumbfounded. It was foreign to me to hear an adult tell a child to fight another. Once I pulled myself together, I risked a conversation with Mom about what I had just heard. I was just honest with her and said I had no way of understanding those "street rules" because I did not grow up that way. I think the mother appreciated the fact that I was honest. She explained that if her daughter did not protect herself, it would be worse for her on the streets because the other kids would see her as weak. She must fight; she had no choice. I thanked the mom for sharing her perspective, but made sure she clearly understood that if her daughter were involved in any fights at school, the daughter would be suspended. The mother said she understood, but that was a consequence she and her daughter would just have to take.

I learned a big lesson that night: that rules differ depending on where you live. I understood that I did not really "get" what life was like for some of my students after they left school. Please don't misunderstand me—

If You Can't Manage Them . . .

I do not believe that students should ever hit each other, nor that schools can ignore issuing consequences if the students choose to do so. However, I did see that some kids are taught rules at home quite different from school rules—and for good reasons. I learned to examine my own attitudes and to realize that I don't have all the answers. I also learned that part of my role as a teacher is to help my students navigate both those worlds, and do so without judgment. Now I work harder to teach them the overt and hidden rules of school while at the same time I accept their culture and traditions.

6. Give them models that look like they do!

In the United States, African American teachers comprise only 6% of the teachers, and of those teachers only 1% are African American males (Kunjufu, 2002). This means that in some schools, too many kids spend an entire year in school without seeing a single adult who looks like them. Therefore, it is critical that you find ways to expose your students to successful professionals who are of their race. Do not underestimate the power of their seeing competent, well-educated people from the community who look like them.

> Too many kids spend an entire year in school without seeing a single adult who looks like them.

In the SOAR program, we invite professional African American people to share their stories of success and give the students a few words of advice. (Please do this in your own classroom, too.) By the end of one year, our

SOAR students had met a doctor, lawyer, real estate agent, entrepreneur, and photographer. It was thrilling to watch them respond and engage with these visitors. Their eyes lit up, their questions were deep, and when the professional left, each student changed his or her future aspirations to the profession that had just been presented. Suddenly, our students could see themselves as achieving something they may not even have dreamed about. Our SOAR kids starting asking (constantly) who was coming next.

7. Let them dream and plan wisely.

One of the major goals of my work with students of color is to help them believe that they are college bound, with a career in mind. What I find as common (especially with boys) is the dream and goal of being a star on a professional sports team. Initially I would respond by giving them the statistics on the likelihood of their becoming a professional athlete. Then I began to realize that it was a waste of my time and their dream. Why should my boys not dream about being a rich, powerful, and admired athlete? It is what they see and hear about every day. When my boys see men that look like them being successful, influential, admired, and revered—who am I to crush that dream?

> Strong relationships with my students of another ethnicity are doubly powerful in breaching the trust gap.

However, I knew I had to help my students learn to plan realistically. Now when a kid says, "I'm going to be an NBA superstar" (especially when he's barely four feet tall), I respond, "Man, that is great! So, what are you doing today to get to college? You do realize that to play in the NBA you must attend college for at least one year, and to play in the NFL you must attend college for two years!" So let's do everything we can to prepare you for college so your dream can become a reality."

> "I think education is freedom. I believe education saved my life."
> – Oprah Winfrey

What I have done is tapped into their "hook." I've shown that I believe in them and their dreams. Eventually (to help the student think about other options), I will add, "What is your backup plan? What will you have in your back pocket if you suffer a career-ending injury?"

I knew this was working when an 8th grade SOAR student introduced himself to a new 7th grader and asked, "What do you plan to do when you get older?" When the 7th grader answered, "I plan to star in the NFL," the older boy had a ready answer. "That's great! But what's your backup plan?" (Needless to say, I grinned with pride from ear to ear!)

• • • • • • • •

Reflect on these ideas in relation to students (and their families) whose ethnicity is different from yours. Take time to consider your own biases, hopes, fears, attitudes, assumptions, goals, and communications with and about these students. The "rules" of the ethnic groups with which you work may be different from those I have discussed in this chapter. You will need to learn the cultural patterns and beliefs for your specific students. Trust them and their parents to help you learn the approaches that will work best in your management style and relationships.

Hook them! Keep them!

SYNCHRONIZED CLASS HOMEWORK DROP

Hooked on Learning

✔

Check the frequency with which you use these strategies to engage students. Add others that you use or would like to use.

Strategy	Often	Some	Rarely
Adding movement			
Adding music			
Adding humor			
Role-play, simulations, dramatizations			
Demonstrations			
Digital or visual design and/or presentations, TED Talks			
Cooperative groups			
Creating shows			
Making models			
Socratic questioning			
Debates			
Songwriting			
Interviews			
Communication tools such as blogs, emails, podcasts, texting, Twitter®, Facebook™, YouTube, Ning, Skype			

Strategy	Often	Some	Rarely
Real-life problems			
Reflections			
Experiments			
Rubrics, graphic organizers			
Students as teachers			
Interactive talks			
Animations			
Games, contests, puzzles, video games			
6-Hat Thinking			
Posters, charts, graphs			
Visual summaries			
Making timelines			
Videoconferencing			
Virtual labs			
Mapping, graphing			
Tech tools for brainstorming, logic, writing, forecasting, mapping			

It's kind of a chicken-and-egg thing—this connection between behavior and effective academic engagement. If you don't have working rules and procedures along with respect and trusting relationships, behavioral issues will seriously disrupt and diminish learning in the classroom. But when preadolescents and adolescents are not engaged in learning, a management nightmare begins. Pencils mysteriously fly across the room. Chatter starts to bounce back and forth at increasing speed. And right before your eyes, things fall apart quickly. (There is no end to the ways kids this age can disrupt the activity when they are not engaged!) In truth, neither management nor engagement comes first. They operate hand in hand. Kids must be "into" the learning all the time—not just with the occasional sparkly lesson or fun field trip—or classroom management will be affected (negatively, I mean)!

One of my colleagues, struggling with classroom management, has asked me, "Why can't they just be students, do what they are supposed to do, and care about learning the way I did?"

Well, the answer is simple: Not all kids are like he was! Not all kids value education the way he did, and not all kids have a mom and a dad at home checking each night on the progress of his homework. Beyond that, not all kids learn the way he did. And furthermore (and this is a BIG one), the world has changed. Beyond differences in learning styles and attitudes, the whole wiring of the brain seems to be different in today's world. The culture, the tools, and the means of gaining and sharing information have changed! With these realities, educators can no longer use the teaching formats that worked for us when we were students.

I find that most students (even the reluctant learners) DO have an intrinsic desire to know new things. There is **something** that excites each student! And it is my job, I believe, to find approaches that hook my students on learning, and keep them on the line!

If You Can't Manage Them . . .

What Is Engagement?

Student engagement is the extent to which a kid identifies with, values, accepts, and participates in learning activities. There is a whole range of factors that contribute to the big picture of engagement. A students' sense of belonging, the relationship with the teacher and other students, and the background he or she brings to school all play a part. But in this chapter, I focus on what the teacher can do in the classroom to hook kids on learning. From my experience, I see that students are engaged by experiences that . . .

- connect with real problems, concerns, interests, and needs in students' lives

- do not feel artificial, contrived, or beneath them

- invite students to meaningfully participate in the learning

- honor and challenge each student's abilities

- include the known components that incite the brain to learn—such things as humor, movement, visual stimulation, music, socializing

I SHOULDN'T HAVE TWEETED THE PLANS FOR MY NEW BIRD HOUSE!

- use the interests, realities, and technological tools that excite and attract them in their real lives and culture

- challenge their imagination and creativity

- push them to use higher-level thinking skills

- give them a choice and voice in their own learning

In his book *No: Why Kids—of All Ages—Need to Hear It and Ways Parents Can Say It,* David Walsh says today's adolescents want information delivered in ways that are fast, fun, and easy (2007, pg. 30). In other words, they might be saying, "Entertain us and we will behave."

I've heard many teachers say, "Well, I didn't sign up to be an entertainer; I signed up to teach." No, we do not need to be entertainers (at least not **all** of the time), but we must present lessons that engage.

Since this is a book on management, there are not enough pages to give all my strategies for hooking kids on learning. Instead, I will share a smattering of ideas in three key areas. I have found that engagement soars and behavioral issues diminish when I do a good job of:

- **getting kids to move,**
- **teaching and using the skills of collaboration,** and
- **incorporating humor.**

There are many wonderful programs and resources to give you more complete "courses" in engagement. Here are a few of my favorites. See the resource list (pages 277–280) for complete citations.

> *Brain/Mind Principles in Action* (Caine, et al.)
>
> *Cooperative Learning* (Kagan)
>
> *Everyone's Invited! Interactive Strategies That Engage Young Adolescents* (Spenser)
>
> *Humor in School Is Serious Business* (Hurren)
>
> *If They Can Argue Well, They Can Write Well* (McBride)
>
> *Teaching Digital Natives* (Prensky)
>
> *The Nuts & Bolts of Active Learning* (Campbell, et al.)

If You Can't Manage Them . . .

Movement

Movement is one of the best ways I know to keep preadolescents and adolescents (especially boys) engaged. Brain-compatible learning principles and a host of other research inform us that students are much more likely to understand well and remember a concept if their bodies are involved in the learning.

I'M DOING THE SEVEN-STEP CHICKEN DANCE!

Brain research also shows that a student can actively listen for only as many minutes as his or her age (Walsh, 2004, pg 33). The days of lecturing for the entire 50-minute class period are over. We now know that even a high-flying, motivated, on-task learner will struggle to absorb information after a stretch of time, because the brain is not functioning at full capacity. I love the oft-repeated quote attributed to P. Dan Wiwchar: "The brain will absorb only what the butt can endure."

Here are some of my favorite ways to keep kids moving:

1. **The seven-step philosophy:** If a student takes seven steps away from and seven steps back to his or her desk—this is enough to get the blood flowing and the brain ready to receive information again (Erlauer, pg 48). Whenever I sense attention wandering or I don't want to be impaled by a flying pencil, I simply say, "Okay, everyone, seven steps from your desk and back."

    At first, the students may think you're crazy and will not participate. Explain why you are doing this and that you expect them to participate. My students quickly learn that when I say, "Seven steps away from your desk,"

I am not asking them—I am directing them. To handle reluctant students, I say in my sly teacher fashion, "Hey, Anna, come here quickly; I need to tell you something." Once she arrives, I remind her of the reasons for doing this and of my expectations. With the brief conversation, I have been direct and specific, strengthened our relationship instead of handing out discipline, and managed to get her to DO the activity!

2. **Lessons in chunks:** Remembering that students can only actively attend for as many minutes as their age, plan to break up your lessons. Anticipate the activity length and include strategies to get them up and moving around. Think about it this way: Create lessons that involve a little bit of you, then a little bit of them, then back to you, then them again, and so on. If you don't move them, preadolescents and adolescents will move you—straight to the funny farm!

3. **Partner up:** Have each student create a Partner Sheet to save the time of choosing partners when you start an activity. Give each student a sheet of paper with six sections, or blocks. Each block contains a word or symbol. The student adds a different partner's name to each block. The word or symbol in each block will be used to identify which partner students will use for a partner activity.

Anytime I need students to move, they get out Partner Sheets; I name a partner block and give

If You Can't Manage Them . . .

them a question, discussion prompt, or other task; and off they go. This is a simple structured way to break up the lesson, allow students to be with their friends, and manage the madness—all in one shot.

4. **Partner puzzles:** Have pairs place large sheets of drawing paper on the floor or wall and create crossword puzzles to review a lesson or concept. There are many Internet sites that can help with this task, if needed.

5. **Choral response with body movements:** Here are some examples: Stomp your feet if you think cells have a nucleus. Grunt if you think the answer to the math problem is correct. Stand up if you believe the war in Iraq was the right decision. Use your foot to point north. Use your head to point south.

6. **Rock, paper, scissors:** Get students out of their seats, use the Partner Sheet to get a partner, play the best of three of this favorite game, then head back to their seats. If another teacher asks me, "What does rock, paper, scissors have to do with learning?" I explain that it has nothing to do with anything, and everything to do with everything! It lets kids relate to each other and is a controlled way to give kids an active break. If they have trouble getting back on task (as some teachers might worry), just stop, repeat the expectations, and remind them that continued inappropriate behavior will end this fun activity. Kids quickly get the point.

If you don't move them, adolescents will move you— straight to the funny farm!

7. **Create a gallery walk:** Write questions on large paper. Post these on walls. In groups of three (each group using a different colored pencil), students discuss, then answer the question or add to the comments written by other students. (Sample question: "Did the United States have to drop the nuclear bomb on Japan to end WWII? Why or why not?")

Management Advice to the Teacher:

If you want to engage kids, don't drone on and on about a topic.

– Kim, grade 8

8. **Silent writing:** Write a question at the top of large chart paper. In groups of three, students visit the chart and respond by writing—NOT talking. They may respond to the question or to what others ahead of them have written.

9. **TAPS (Think Aloud Problem Solve):** Assign letter A to one partner and letter B to another. Pose a question. Partner A will answer for 30 seconds while Partner B only listens. Partner B can nod the head, but not talk. Switch places. Partner B talks and A listens. At the end, call on anyone. That person must share his or her answers or the comments of the partner.

10. **The last word:** Create groups of three. Each student becomes an A, B, or C. Pose a question. Partner A responds aloud for 30 seconds. B has 40 seconds to respond to what A said and add his or her perspective. C does the same for 40 seconds. Finally, A gets to respond to B and C for 40 seconds.

If You Can't Manage Them . . .

11. **Board games:** Create games that teach or review your content. Put the directions on the back and let students figure out how to play. All you have to do is hand them out and walk around making sure students are playing. Laminate the game boards for next year. (Lamination—a teacher's best friend!)

12. **Rap-a-summary:** This tactic gets kids moving while it engages them in content that is real and relevant. I bring pertinent current event stories and issues for students to discuss. I carefully choose those that I know will pique their interest. After the discussion, I ask students to create a rap that summarizes the issue. Or, I take them to this website to rap and dance along with a rap-style summary of the week: *www.weekinrap.com.*

Collaboration

> My kids retain ideas when they are presented with variety, high-interest, and humor.
> – Anne, middle school parent

We know that middle and high school students love to be with their friends every moment of every day. Most kids will tell you it's the reason they come to school. (Here all this time we thought it was our intellectual stimulation that brought them back each day!) And most teachers realize that there are great benefits to cooperative groups: interdependence, purposeful interaction, increase in social skills (communication, decision making, cooperation, leadership), enhanced self-esteem, empowerment for students, and improved relationships. What's more, a growing body of research tells us that kids learn more when they work collaboratively. Understandings are deepened by the interaction.

So why are teachers scared of groups? (I was!) Quite simply, it's because we think we can't control students in them. Some groups are not academically productive. Some groups can't settle into the work; they just want to chat. Some students do nothing and let the other group members do the work. Although we know it's a good thing for students, we often move away from collaboration because of the potential problems.

The good news is that you **can** train middle and high school students to work well in groups. But it does take planning and deliberate effort to make sure the students are doing what the teacher intends them to do.

I hope you'll investigate the pros on cooperative learning (Kagan, 1994; Johnson & Johnson, 1994; and Slavin, 1994) to learn how to do this process well. I share here some strategies that have worked for me to make groups an effective instructional tool and not another adolescent social encounter or management problem:

1. **Create groups carefully.** The time you take upfront to create groups helps all aspects of group dynamics tremendously and reduces management issues. When you create the groups, you force students to work with those students they do not know as well. This goes a long way toward building relationships and community within your class. It also is great practice for the future when they must work with people they do not know or may

not like. Many times I purposefully put strong leaders together specifically to teach students how to work in groups with a plethora of personalities, styles, and attitudes. It can be quite interesting—I must say!

Group work fosters creativity.

Group gifted with gifted, homogeneous, heterogeneous, and so on. Allow students to be in a group with others that share ethnicity—especially if there are very few in your class. Don't be afraid, at times, to put your unmotivated students in a group as well. Now *that* presents an interesting dilemma for a group of students who have learned to lean on their classmates to complete a project or assignment!

2. **Limit group size.** Make every effort to create groups **no larger than three.** With more, there is often not enough for each person to do. With pairs, there is not a broad enough base of knowledge or perspective. With four, often one member gets left out. Try different sized groups once students get good at group work.

3. **Arrange students facing each other.** Group members **must** be in a circle—knee to knee and eye to eye. If students sit on the floor, they should still work in a circle, knee to knee.

4. **Teach students how to function in a group.** Clearly explain all expectations and ground rules for group work. Remind students that all the usual class expectations will be in effect. Practice good listening skills by doing activities such as TAPS (Think Aloud Problem Solve) described on page 243.

5. **Plan for individual accountability and group accountability.** Each member of the group must have a responsibility that can be assessed by the teacher. For example, Member 1: present; Member 2: write a paragraph; Member 3: create a PowerPoint. Group accountability could focus on how well they did what was expected. (All raised hand, all helped with project, and so on.)

6. **Set a procedure for teacher-answered questions.** I suggest that the teacher not answer questions unless all members of the group raise hands together. This forces members to rely on each other to do the task. They go to the teacher for help when the whole group decides to do this. (You might add this to your behavioral rubric as a way to help ensure that it happens.)

Management Advice to the Teacher:

If you want to engage kids, give them choices about what they learn.

– Cassandra, grade 7

7. **Constantly monitor group behavior.** You absolutely cannot stay at your desk while students work in groups. Be visible—constantly reminding students of the expectations. Keep moving. (Think of this as your own weight loss program!) A colleague of mine realized that she seemed to be drawn to her laptop when students were working in groups. This became a horrible habit, and management

If You Can't Manage Them . . .

problems piled up. Thinking creatively, she decided to walk around, quietly playing her guitar. Her tactic solved the management issues and deepened relationships—particularly with students who shared her love of the guitar.

8. **Give immediate feedback.** Give students a response (the same day, if possible) about their group behavior and accomplishments. Students need to be taught how to function in groups. Immediate feedback gives them the opportunity to change behavior and earn more points the very next day.

9. **Include individual reflections.** Do this every time. Sometimes with group work, only a few of the students are actually doing the work and learning about the topic. When students reflect on their own, I can tell if they are actively involved in the group work, how they feel about the group process, and what they have learned. Individuals might write a brief summary of what they learned about the topic that day, create a timeline of the topic's major events, make a bubble map answering Who? What? Why? When? or Where? for the topic, or create questions about the main ideas they discovered.

10. **Include a behavioral component in the assessment rubric.** When you create your rubric to evaluate the group work and process, include a few items that address individual behavior. See examples on the right.

> __ Student remains with group at all times. (2 pts)
>
> __ Student is on task at all times. (2 pts)
>
> __ Student followed instructions and did not ask questions already discussed or presented in class by the teacher. (2 pts)

Humor

If you work with preadolescents and adolescents, humor must be a part of your tool kit. (It's clearly needed for survival.) When you stop and think about it, we really are so lucky to work with kids of this age span. At what other level does a teacher get to have a personal reality show play out before his or her eyes day after day after day? Seriously, do we ever truly know what is going to happen from one day to the next?

In my class the other day, we were discussing a current event that involved a young person who nearly drowned after falling through the ice. I asked the class, "What do experts say you should do if you fall through the ice?"

I expected some answer about tactics to follow to keep from going under the ice. Instead, Janie proudly raised her hand and said, "Hold your breath." (The scary part of this is that Janie was a part of our gifted-talented program.)

On the night of our school Open House, an eighth grade boy decided to greet our parents by twirling two tampons in the air while shouting, "Welcome to West!" What was he thinking (or not thinking)? As I pulled him into the office, I asked, "Tony, do you do things like this often?"

He looked at me and said, "Well, Ms. C, yes, but only on my own time." ("Well, that's a relief!" I thought.)

Oh, the things kids this age do and say! If you aren't laughing at least five times a day, you are not listening or observing well. (And you might think about finding a new grade level to teach.)

If You Can't Manage Them . . .

Great teachers of preadolescents and adolescents understand the need for appropriate humor, enjoy it, participate in it, look for opportunities to include it, use it to their advantage, and are never afraid to laugh with students or at themselves.

Laughter relaxes the body, relieves stress and tension, and promotes a sense of well-being. I asked 100 parents this question in an email: "What teacher characteristics or behaviors are connected to successful learning for your child?" Most included "a sense of humor" or "makes learning fun" as a part of their response. Few things engage students as quickly and reliably as humor. It can be a wonderful tool if used wisely. Even if you are not naturally funny, you can still have a sense of humor and find ways to bring humor into your classroom.

Some Ways to Use Humor

Here are some ways to use humor in your classroom to engage student attention and warm the learning atmosphere. Remember, though: Never try to be or act in any way you are not. Only use strategies with which you are comfortable.

- Use appropriate humor to defuse behavioral situations. For example: So often when two kids are in some altercation, one will say, "Ms. C, Marcus is picking on me." Based on the relationship I have created with each of these students and based on what I observe, I may respond by saying, "Really? I can see why!" And then, of course, I smile and tell them I'm kidding.

- Don't be afraid to make fun of yourself and laugh at yourself. I start every year by sharing a story about my thumbs. I inform students that I am about to tell them something about myself that I am embarrassed to share, but I think they should know. (Watch them perk up in their seats.) I tell them that something went terribly wrong with my thumbs and they look like big toes. (They are really perking up now.) I go on to caution them that they might have nightmares after they see these thumbs—but that I hope they will learn to accept me for who I am—thumbs and all. Then I show my thumbs; I even invite them to come up and get a closer look, and, if they ask, allow them to touch them. Oh, my goodness, do we have a laugh!

• • • • I went to observe a colleague who takes his subject (math) and his job very seriously. While waiting for class to start, two students said, "Mr. Bentley, we are waiting for our joke today." Bentley, a solemn young man, proceeded to tell the lamest joke on the planet. The students hooted and howled while he laughed a sincere and deep belly laugh.

During the post-observation meeting, I asked if he really thought his jokes were funny. His answer was, "Well, not all of them, but the kids love it. We laugh, they complain, and the class settles in for the day." He says he starts every day with a joke, and the worse the joke—the better it is for the class. He's not a real funny person outside of class, but he has found a way to make his students laugh.

• • • • YouTube® gives you a great way to bring funny stories into the classroom. Try this source in the YouTube search engine for appropriate material—some great stories: Steve Hartman Assignment America . . . . Using YouTube clips connects with kids because you are using one of their favorite genres. I also allow students to give me ideas of funny Youtube clips they have seen and think I should

> Management Advice to the Teacher:
>
> **If you want to engage kids, have fun activities that aren't lame or weird.**
> – Kyrsten, grade 8

If You Can't Manage Them . . .

show in class. (Remember, NEVER show the clip until you have seen it first. Trust me, I have learned the hard way!)

- • • • Tongue twisters are such fun. Look them up. Make them up. The Internet is a great source. Here are two of my favorite sites—one English, the second one Spanish:
http://www.indianchild.com/tongue_twisters.htm
http://www.lexiophiles.com/english/tongue-twisters-in-spanish

- • • • When my students need a break, I use an activity called "What You Got?" I simply ask students who can do something funny with their body. ("Can anyone touch your nose with your tongue, wiggle your ears, raise one eyebrow, or such?") Be prepared! You are going to witness some wild things!

Some Ways NOT to Use Humor

I've spoken about **appropriate** use of humor. That's because if used without thought, wisdom, and compassion, humor can harm.

- • • • Never use humor to put down a student for any reason. It will simply backfire on you. And the other students in the class will view you as not being safe or kind.

- • • • Be very perceptive when you try to joke around with a student. Watch the child's body language and other nonverbal signs that this particular student does not appreciate your joke or humor. If this happens, reassure the student that you were just trying to have fun. Tell the student that you apologize if he or she felt offended or upset. Remember that, at their stage of brain development, preadolescents and adolescents may have difficulty differentiating between subtle humor and literal meanings.

- • • • Likewise, when you joke around with an individual, be perceptive of class reaction. Do the students laugh and then let it go? Or do you see and hear students making references several minutes later? If this happens, your joking was a huge mistake. Stop the class for a moment and correct the mistake by explaining that your intent was simply to inject a bit of humor but not to embarass the individual and not to fuel a disruption of the class. Apologize for the misstep if you sense this will help bring the class back to order.

  A few years ago I had one of my toughest classes ever. Unbeknownst to me, the most terrible bully of my career was in that class. As I was developing relationships with the students, I joked around with a student who I thought could handle it. I was clearly mistaken. After I joked with him, there was a feeding frenzy—led by the bully. It soon became clear that joking around with any student in that class was dangerous. The bully saw it as permission to joke with the students, too—only his joking was cruel. It was a difficult, but valuable lesson for me to learn.

- • • • Do not confuse sarcasm with humor. There is absolutely no room in a classroom for sarcasm. Students at this age, no matter how bright they are, will struggle to understand what you are saying and will generally feel the sarcasm as negative. Sarcasm is a passive-aggressive tool—never an effective management or teaching strategy.

If You Can't Manage Them . . .

Experienced teachers have picked up this simple skill—the ability to quickly recognize when students are losing their focus and are no longer engaged. Good managers wrap up the activity or pull out an engaging strategy to help students refocus. Remember that a student who is not engaged is a student looking for ways to be engaged. The engagement he or she chooses might spell disaster for any learning or for peace in the classroom.

If you are going to keep students engaged, you cannot be afraid to try new things—to step out of your comfort zone. I tell myself and the teachers I mentor, "I am not afraid to fail. I am more afraid not to try." So, give it a go, try something new, laugh when it goes wrong, applaud yourself when it goes well. But for all your students out there, please try something!

> **Happy students learn better.**
> – Jan, middle school parent

Remember the email question to parents I mentioned earlier? An astounding percentage of the parents mentioned that success for their students was connected to the teacher's passion for the subject. This is part of Student Engagement 101. Your enthusiasm about the material is contagious. If you are having trouble keeping kids engaged—check your own passion level.

Finally, think of it this way: Better engagement = fewer discipline problems = increase in motivation = better performance! In the end, this is what we were hired to do.

Chapter 12

Real-Life Discipline Scenarios

What would YOU do?

What I Would Do

Write notes about how you would handle each scenario on pages 257 through 260.

Scenario 1

Scenario 2

Scenario 3

Scenario 4

Scenario 5

Scenario 6

Scenario 7

Scenario 8

Scenario 9

Scenario 10

The unpredictability of the adolescent is one of the most exciting (and challenging) factors in the school lives of their teachers. One moment all systems are a "go," and within minutes the situation is near chaos.

As the final chapter, I present a variety of real management scenarios. Consider how you would handle each situation (taking into account the ideas of the book). Keep in mind that you will have a tendency to be affected by your past experiences with conflict. If you struggle with conflict situations, the solution may involve pushing yourself out of your comfort zone. The good news is that as your experience increases, many classroom situations will seem less hectic and more manageable.

Read Scenarios 1–10. Write down a few ideas about what you might do to address each situation. (Use the form on page 256.) Later in the chapter I will explain what I tried and how it worked—so you can compare your notes to my experience! Have fun! This should inspire a lot of creative thinking and discussion with colleagues (or even with students).

Scenario #1

You have a middle school class of mostly boys—one of whom is a full-blown bully. Kids are terrified of him and do just about anything to gain his approval (or avoid his wrath). Every time anyone in the class says something that the bully deems "stupid," he makes a sound, laughs, or rolls his eyes. Quickly the other students follow his lead and join in. He is brilliant at recognizing how far he can push the teacher. He is quick to say he is sorry and that it won't happen again. (Side note: His parents think the school is out to get him.) **What do you do?**

Scenario #2

During a short lecture (inspiring, I'm sure!) and discussion with your class, one student decides to play the class clown and make funny comments. At first you find it funny, but as the discussion progresses, the clown refuses to stop. This is a very popular student who many times does liven up the class. You redirect her or him several times. But the behavior continues. **What do you do?**

THIS MIGHT BE OVER THE TOP, MICHAEL!

Scenario #3

Several students continue to show up to class without a textbook, pencil, or paper. You tell them to come prepared the next day or to expect a consequence: a lunch detention with you. The next day, none of them is prepared. **What do you do?**

Scenario #4

During group work, one group is continually off-task— not doing what they are supposed to do. You approach the group several times. Finally, one student reports, "Davon won't do anything; all he does is screw around."

Davon announces loudly that this is not true. All of a sudden, the entire group is complaining. (Side note: Davon is diagnosed with mild Asperger's syndrome. One of his IEP goals is to learn to work productively with peers.) **What do you do?**

Scenario #5

As you are facilitating a class conversation on a content subject, a cell phone rings or beeps. **What do you do?**

Scenario #6

During a class discussion, the topic of bullying comes up (unrelated to the subject at hand). Seeing the lively interest in this topic, you conclude that it is more important at this moment than the stages of mitosis. So you ask students what they think teachers need to know about bullying in your school. You go on to ask, "If you were to make a list of the top three girl bullies and the top three boy bullies in your grade, would the names be the same on every list?" (Notice that this is a hypothetical—"IF you were to make." You did not have the students actually make a list.) Student answers are overwhelmingly "YES." You see this as one of those great educational moments for you and your students.

Later that day, you get word that some students have been going around saying that they did make the list in your class and that so-and-so students are on it. One girl even tells another girl that her name is at the top of the list. That evening, unbeknownst to you, the principal receives parent phone calls about this list. The next morning, the girl who is said to be at the top of the list is waiting in your room with her father. **What do you do?**

Scenario #7

You are a white teacher with a class of mostly white students. A few students are Hispanic or African American. You ask one black student to sit down and start on his work. The student turns around and says, in front of the class, "You're a racist and never tell the white kids to sit down!" **What do you do?**

If You Can't Manage Them . . .

Scenario #8

You have a group of really chatty girls. They seem to think they can talk whenever they want, and do so on a regular basis. These particular girls are very popular and smart, and are leaders within your class. When your principal observes the class, he tells you that the chatty behavior needs to stop. He promises to visit you again next week, and says he will be specifically looking for strategies you've implemented to address this behavior. **What do you do?**

> Management Advice to the Teacher:
> **Don't just keep going on and on when students are chatting.**
> – Chrisna, grade 7

Scenario #9

A student is extremely defiant in class. Every time you redirect this individual, out comes an insolent comment and a refusal to work. Finally you have had enough. You tell the student to go to the office. The student refuses to move. You ask again. The student tells you to go to ____, and does not move. **What do you do?**

Scenario #10

One of your homework assignments requires the students to do a short activity with an adult (someone 18 or older). The next day, you get an email from a very upset parent explaining that it is your job, not hers, to be the teacher. She goes on to say that she does not have time to do homework with her child and thinks the activity is a waste of time. You notice that the parent has copied the principal and superintendent on the email. **What do you do?**

If You Can't Manage Them . . .

260

What I Tried

Here are my responses to the previous situations. These are strategies I thought would work. Your ideas may be different. This does not mean that yours are wrong and mine are right. As you read, you will find that not all of my responses were successful. In some cases, my strategies made things worse! You can compare your solutions with mine, and perhaps draw some conclusions that you'll have ready if such a scenario becomes reality for you!

• • • • Scenario #1

This difficult situation has me scratching my head to this day. I still have never encountered a bully as mean and vicious as that kid I had every day in Block 3. My challenge was to protect the class from this bully. At the same time, it was my job to teach the bully, too. I decided to call his third grade teacher for her insights. As my instincts told me, he had been a bully since kindergarten. ("Great!" I'm thinking—with dread.) She cautioned that trying to reason with or help him see what he was doing would not work. She shared some strategies that she had found workable for a period of time. One was to make sure he clearly understood that the teacher was not afraid of him. (I was thinking to myself, "But I think I AM afraid of him!")

Next, I talked to his sixth grade teacher who advised me: "Privately, not publicly, tell him you know he is a bully and that you will not allow that behavior in your classroom." Since he had been (and still was) a master at not getting caught by the teacher, she suggested I seat him as close to me as possible. (I must say I was hoping she

DON'T MAKE ME DO SOMETHING YOU'RE GOING TO REGRET.

If You Can't Manage Them . . .

would suggest seating him in the hall or in another county!) She told me to position myself close to him during group work and not take my eyes off him. Her advice was right on: I turned my back on him one day. In a flash, another member of his group had gum stuck in her hair. I knew the bully had done this; so did everyone else. But I could not prove it. Getting testimony from other kids would have been fruitless. They were terrified of him.

> My challenge was to protect the class from this bully. At the same time, it was my job to teach the bully, too.

According to his previous teachers, the bully's parents blamed the school and teachers for their son's behavior. So basically, this kid was constantly in my sight for an entire school year. I consistently redirected him when needed. I knew it was a must for him and the other students to understand that I would not allow or ignore this behavior. We survived the year—and I am still standing (and teaching)!

Scenario #2

Ahhhh—the infamous "class clown syndrome." Every school has clowns. They tend to be males. Sometimes they are so charming and funny that they are hard to manage. I was the class clown all through junior high and high school, so I understood what he was trying to accomplish. I decided to do with this young man what I wished a teacher had done with me—not squelch my humor, but rather teach me when its use was (and was not) appropriate.

In this situation, the task was to refocus the class. So I said, "Andre, I need you to stop with the remarks, now. One more time and you are out in the hall."

Andre obviously did not think I was serious. He cracked another joke, and I had no choice but to send him to the hall. The hallway conversation was my time to help Andre understand how to read clues to recognize when it is time to stop the clowning. I asked if he had noticed when I started getting frustrated with his remarks. He said, "Maybe," but wasn't sure.

I gave him concrete examples of how my voice and facial expressions changed. I emphasized that he should learn to read his audience. I promised Andre that the next time he started to cross the line I would give him a signal that it's time to stop. Hey, it worked! Andre continued to be the class clown, but began to understand when enough was enough.

Scenario #3

This was an easy one. This was a clear class rule and I had specified consequences. I spoke to each student, reminding that I expected him or her to come to class prepared and they had not. To show consistent follow-through, each of them was assigned lunch detention.

Scenario #4

Although Davon needed to learn to work with peers, it seemed that some issue would arise whenever I put him in a group. Within minutes the group would fall apart, with Davon somehow in the mix. I consulted his case manager and my colleagues, and still could not find the answer.

So I decided to call his parents. Right away, I told them that Davon was not in trouble, but that I needed their help and advice. I explained the situation. I simply asked them what insights they could give to assist my efforts to help their son work with his peers. I asked what worked for them at home.

They said that Davon had long had difficulty with groups. Mom explained that working in groups increased his anxiety and impulsivity, which in turn made him act in annoying ways (an understatement, I thought!).

She suggested I make a rule that if he disrupted the group during his five minutes, I'd add a minute to his group time. I tried the parents' suggestions. They worked. It was not perfect, but it was much, much better for everyone. Parents know their child better than anyone. Don't hesitate to ask for their help.

> Parents know their child better than anyone. Don't hesitate to ask for their help.

• • • • Scenario #5

Cell phones ringing, students texting in class—technology has added a new dimension to classroom management! Personally, I do not get wigged out about cell phones or texting. I certainly address it, but I seldom take phones away unless I have promised to do so as a consequence for their being used in class again. (You may feel differently—and that is okay!) If I am concerned about texting, I have all students place phones on their desks in a certain spot where I can see them. Cell phones stay there until the end of class.

One day a phone started ringing in my class. This girl, sitting in the front row, was a straight A student—a rule follower. She never (I repeat—never) got into trouble. When her phone rang, she dove to the floor to dig in her purse, grabbed the phone, and handed it to me while it was still ringing. I answered it and heard, "Amy, this is Grandpa. I'm going to be late to your softball game tonight."

I said, "Hello, Grandpa, this is Amy's teacher and she's in class right now."

I hoped he would get the message, but he continued. "Well, could you tell Amy that Grandma and Grandpa will be a little late?" I told Grandpa (with a chuckle) that for me to give Amy the message I would need a Reese's Peanut Butter Blizzard. That afternoon when Grandpa came to the softball game, he stopped by my room with some yummy ice cream!

So I say don't *take* the phones; *answer* their phones! Seriously, the class had a great laugh and saw me as flexible and understanding. You see, I trusted that this would never happen again for Amy, and it didn't.

In my district, students are bussed in from places that can be very dangerous, particularly when they are getting off the bus in the dark. A cell phone may be the only connection to their families, and in some cases their small piece of comfort and safety. It's certainly okay to take the cell phone during school, but let them have it to take home.

If your school has a cell phone policy requiring parents to pick up the phone when rules are not followed, take care in logging an offense. Many parents don't have transportation or time to come in and pick up a cell phone. A policy could give a choice: A parent picks it up, or the student checks it in at the office each

THIS IS PROBABLY NOT WHAT THE TEACHER MEANT BY GROUP WORK.

If You Can't Manage Them . . .

morning and picks it up at the end of the day for a week. Tell students you expect them to follow cell phone rules. At the same time, let them know that you love them enough to understand their need for their phones.

• • • • Scenario #6

To be clear: I did not have the students make the list. I almost did, but my gut told me not to. (Thank goodness I was listening.) Come to find out, this so-called list became the talk of many parents—all calling each other to decide what to do about it.

Eventually, the principal and I discovered that the girl who showed up at my door with her father turned out to be bully number one in our school. In class she was an absolute angel. I never would have guessed her to be on the list. (See how much we teachers *don't* know?) But outside class she was the leader of a major clique of girls that chose who was "in" and who was "out. " Some girls took our class conversation as permission to finally go after the bully. I think they really felt that I "had their backs" and this made them feel safe to unleash on her. Unleash they did, saying that her name was at the top of the list, that "Ms. C now knows, and now she doesn't like you, either." They even went so far as to tell her that they had posted the list of girl bullies on Facebook™.

Her lawyer dad wanted me to know what was happening to his daughter. I apologized profusely, reassuring both that there was no list and it was a mistake even to mention the idea.

> *Sometimes the best tactic is to "leave bad enough alone."*

My mistake put ideas into the heads of my students, and from there it went crazy. I spoke to my principal at length about whether or not I should assure all my students there was no list. We realized that they would hear what they wanted to hear. We decided not to discuss the list again. Sometimes the best tactic is to "leave bad enough alone."

• • • • Scenario #7

Being called a racist is one of the worst things that can happen to an educator. As a white teacher with nonwhite students, I know that I do everything I can **not** to behave in any racially discriminatory ways. In the face of such an accusation, the instinct is to be defensive, to deny, or to respond as if the student just cut off your right arm. I do believe that our communities and classrooms are not free of racist beliefs. I observe that many racist feelings have gone undercover and show themselves in subtle ways. Many of us choose not to talk about racism, or certainly hope it does not exist.

If you're accused, I suggest you take a deep breath and say simply, "I'm sorry you feel that way. It is not my intention to be racist, but let's you and I talk about that later." This alone usually defuses the situation. Such a response validates the student's feelings, but does not give the reaction they are accustomed to receiving. In addition, it lets that student and all students know that you are willing to talk about the accusation with the student when he or she is calm (and you are over the shock).

I encourage you to risk talking to any student who accuses you of racism. Maybe the student perceived what you did as racist, maybe it really was racist, or maybe the student was just angry and tossed out the racist comment. In any case, a discussion is a valuable experience for both the teacher and the student. If you are uncomfortable having such a discussion alone with the student, ask your guidance counselor to mediate. Please do not miss an opportunity to learn, simply because you are afraid of what you might hear.

Scenario #8

When your principal speaks—listen. In this instance, a new teacher asked me for advice about what to do with these chatty girls. This kind of situation is tricky. You do not want to squelch student enthusiasm or leadership. Yet the incessant talking interferes with the learning of all the students. This teacher had already tried various techniques, but the girls would roll their eyes, laugh, and start talking again within minutes.

We decided to try a behavioral rubric that focused on these particular behaviors. We knew these girls valued their grades, so we worked on a rubric where better behavior would increase their participation points. These were the rubric items:

___ Students will not talk when the teacher or their peers have the floor. (5 pts)

___ Students will not roll their eyes or demonstrate other disrespectful actions if they are redirected. (5 pts)

At the next observation, her principal was delighted to see the use of the behavior rubric, and happily noted this good start at taking concrete steps to improve the girls' behavior.

Scenario #9

Basically, this situation is a major power struggle brewing between teacher and student. The student has likely put herself or himself in a corner they'd rather not be in, but must save face. When this happened to me, I walked over and whispered this in the student's ear: "I know

THE TEACHER GIVES CARLA A WAY TO SAVE FACE.

you don't want this any more than I do, so I'm going to give you 20 seconds to walk out of this room. If you need to, take a few seconds to save face. But if you choose not to leave, you have left me no choice but to call the office and have you physically removed. You can do this."

Then I simply walked away. The young lady took at least 15 seconds to save face, then got up and left. Later in the day, I met with her and the assistant principal to discuss what had happened and how we expected that not to happen again.

Scenario #10

I must say it is terribly frustrating to have a parent copy an email to the principal and superintendent before you have had a chance to respond; but trust me—this *does* happen! In this case, my first reaction was surprise and confusion. I thought my

If You Can't Manage Them . . .

assignment was a wise one—a great way for parent and student to bond over something related to school.

I failed to consider that some parents do not have the time, energy, or desire for such a task. Perhaps a parent feels incompetent to help with homework. Perhaps the parent works nights and just is not able to do this. Sometimes parents and kids become adversaries when doing homework together. Or, like this parent, he or she may believe it is the teacher's job to teach and the parent's job to parent.

Management Advice to the Teacher:

If you do not face a problem and move to take charge—there will be trouble!

– Quincy, grade 8

Please know that I have not dropped the idea of kids working on homework with an adult. I have modified it so that they can work with any family member or adult. (If an adult is not available, the student can teach a younger or older sibling.) Of course, I have **never** asked the adult to teach a new concept. Instead, I give assignments where students have to teach an adult about something learned in class. Second, I extend the assignment over a few days so the student has time to work with an adult. Third, I give students permission to be excused from the assignment—no questions asked. Finally, I communicate the assignment to parents by email or website so they know it is coming and are prepared to ask about it. Very few students have ever asked to be excused from such an assignment.

Management is *SO* every day!

When it comes to classroom management, I am certain of this: You will always have to "manage"—every day, every class. Some teachers think that once they have established expectations and built relationships with their students, things will sail along smoothly. Not so! Directing and redirecting kids is always there!

In recent years, class sizes have exploded. I am constantly trying to figure out ways to keep a lot of students engaged and moving in appropriate directions at the same time. Once routines are established, relationships are created, lessons are organized, and my confidence as a teacher is strong, disruptions will lessen. My classroom will run smoothly (mostly). Even so, I remind myself each school day that I will be "managing the mob" today—that this is part of my job and critical to learning.

Good Managers—Born or Bred?

As you can tell, my central message is that you can learn to be an effective manager if you are willing to change your behaviors to meet the needs of the students you have before you. I have seen teachers at all levels of experience make changes and improve. My sister struggled to manage her sixth graders. Her principal gave her one year to turn things around in the area of classroom management. Today she is in her 28th year as a successful educator. One of my colleagues moved from elementary music to middle school music and was faced with striking differences when it

If You Can't Manage Them . . .

came to managing her choir room. Two years later, she is thriving as our music teacher. How did she do it? First, she recognized that her previous management style would not work with middle school students. Then she read books on classroom management, looked for help, took some risks, tried different suggestions, and became more direct.

The notion that classroom managers are born is only partially correct. If you are naturally direct and unafraid of conflict, this may be easier for you. But anyone who is willing to take a risk can learn the skill of good management. Just be open to change and resist the temptation to blame the students, parents, and society.

Ready for Day One?

This catchy quote (on the right) can certainly apply to your first day with your students. Every student who enters your classroom on that first day is watching you, deciding what kind of a teacher you will be, wondering what they can get away with, and most certainly, sizing you up as a classroom manager. Are you ready for the challenge? I think you are!

"You never get a second chance to make a first impression."
– Unknown

As you approach that first day, keep in mind the strategies and techniques you have read about in this book:

- Do you know your bottom line?
- Are you ready to define and model respect and disrespect? How, specifically, will you demonstrate these?
- What expectations will you immediately establish?

- What will you do if a student violates one of your expectations?
- What sequence or steps will you use to alert a student to his or her unacceptable behavior?
- What consequences will you administer?
- What will be your progression of consequences?
- Are you ready to follow through with consequences?

Consider these questions also:

- How do you deal with conflict? Will you avoid it at all costs? Will you joke? Will you ignore the infraction? Or will you take consistent steps to administer a consequence and follow through?

- How will you plan your first day's lessons? How will students be able to move into an activity? Are you confident about how you will end each activity and have the students settle down again?

- Do you have enough planned to get through the first day? You will be nervous and will move very quickly through your material. I still over-plan Day One—and I've been doing this for 18 years! Over plan, baby, over plan!

TONY, LAST SEPTEMBER, I EXPLAINED THE EXPECTATIONS ABOUT GUM-CHEWING. WHY DO I NEED TO TELL YOU AGAIN IN MARCH?

- How will you begin building relationships with your students? How will you tell them that you are their leader and not their buddy?

If You Can't Manage Them . . .

- - - • Have you begun adding items to your list of things to do for the next day? You can be sure some students will test you on Day Two to see if you meant what you said on the first day!

After I presented a workshop on classroom management in late fall, I received this email from an attendee: "Why didn't somebody teach me this stuff in August—not November? If I had known from the start how to be consistent and follow through, I would have had fewer discipline problems."

Show that you are the leader of your classroom from Day One—not from Day Twelve. You can't really do Day One or Day Two over! Think of it this way: A 100-meter track athlete sits in the block and says to herself, "Well, I'll just smile and be nice to the runners around me, and maybe they'll like me and let me win!" (Do I need to say more?)

Beyond Days One & Two

Anyone who is willing to take a risk can learn the skills of good management.

Remember, you can be firm, direct, and consistent and still have kids like you and, most important, respect you. Do this every day! There's an old adage in the educational world that says, "Never smile until winter break." I think that's rubbish, but I certainly would be firm, consistent, and follow through on all the days of your teaching life!

There's another adage in education: "Once you lose control, it will be nearly impossible to get it back." (Now *this* one, I almost believe!) But I **do** want to say—Don't give up! The absolute best approach is to start well on Day One, but I have seen teachers make great strides in management at many times during the year. So if you get off to a poor start, do your best to start over right away. Do not wait until next year!

Nurture Your Support System

Working with preadolescents and adolescents is an honor—I really believe that. But, wow, it can be tough! As my final advice, I encourage you to build a network of others to join in your efforts to do the best for students.

One Check in with a student's former teachers.

I will often contact an elementary teacher to learn what strategies he or she found successful with a particular child or family. With this tactic, I have gained many valuable insights and saved myself a lot of wasted time and trouble.

Two Ask your colleagues for help.

If you were having a technology problem, would you be afraid to ask for help? Probably not! But lots of teachers don't want to talk or share struggles about management with fellow teachers. Yet we know management difficulties have a huge impact on our teaching! I urge you to discuss management issues openly with your team or other colleagues. Don't be afraid to ask a principal, assistant principal, or veteran teacher for guidance. Identify a successful

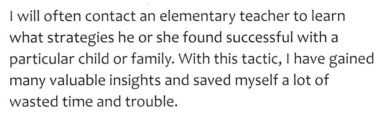

Observe a Colleague

Watch for:
- Routines & procedures
- How the teacher starts the class
- Techniques used to build relationships with students
- How transitions are managed
- Consistencies or inconsistencies
- Specific effective management strategies
- Techniques you would like to try

If You Can't Manage Them . . .

teacher and observe that colleague in action. The management techniques, particularly those seen in the first 10 minutes of class, will provide you with a bucket load of ideas, techniques, and strategies.

Three **Build trusting relationships with parents.**

Communicate regularly with parents; share information by email, newsletters, notes, and your class website. See to it that you have positive contacts with all parents—sharing positive messages about their children. Don't let a discipline problem be the occasion for your first contact with any parent. If you work at good relationships with parents, you will have them on-board to work with you when there is a problem.

Four **Listen to your students.**

My best teachers sit in front of me every day. What better way to learn than from those who are directly affected by our management style? Talk to your students. Ask them for feedback. LISTEN to the valuable insights they offer!

Want to be an effective manager? Take time to talk with your students.

– Sara, middle school teacher

I wish you success, energy, patience, and consistency as you hone your skills at living and working with students. I believe you CAN manage them—and you CAN teach them!

Resources

Adler, A. (1956). *The individual psychology of Alfred Adler: A systematic presentation in selections from his writings.* New York, NY: Harper & Row.

Adler, N. (2002). Interpretations of the meaning of care: Creating caring relationships in urban middle school classrooms. *Urban Education, 37(2),* March, 241–266.

Anderman, E. M., Maehr, M. L., & Midgley, C. (1999). Declining motivation after the transition to middle school: Schools can make a difference. *Journal of Research and Development in Education, 32(3),* 131–147.

Bender, W. L. (2003). *Relational discipline: Strategies for in-your-face students.* Boston, MA: Pearson. (Note: A revised edition was published by Information Age Publishing in 2007).

Bennis, W. (1994). *On becoming a leader.* New York, NY: Perseus. (Note: A revised edition was published by Basic Books in 2009).

Bernstein, N. (1996). *Treating the unmanageable adolescent: A guide to oppositional defiant and conduct disorders.* Northvale, NJ: Jason Aronson.

Birch, S. H., & Ladd, G. W. (1998). Children's interpersonal behaviors and the teacher–child relationship. *Developmental Psychology, 35(5),* 934–946.

Bondy, E., & Ross, D. D. (2008). The positive classroom: The teacher as warm demander. *Educational Leadership, 66(1),* 54–58.

Brophy, J. E. (1996). *Teaching problem students.* New York, NY: Guilford.

Brophy, J. E., & McCaslin, N. (1992). Teachers' reports of how they perceive and cope with problem students. *Elementary School Journal, 93(1),* 3–68.

Bryk, A. S., & Schneider, B. (2002). *Trust in schools: A core resource for improvement.* New York, NY: Russell Sage Foundation.

Buckelew, M. (2000). Parent homework bridges the student–teacher gap. *The Voice, 5(1),* 7, 19.

Caine, C., Caine. G., McClintock, C., & Klimek, K. (2005). *12 Brain/mind principles in action.* Thousand Oaks, CA: Corwin Press. (Note: The 2nd edition was published in 2009).

Campbell, K., et al. (2009). *The nuts & bolts of active learning.* Nashville, TN: Incentive Publications.

Campbell, K., & Wahl, K. (2009). *A handbook for closing the achievement gap: SOAR.* Nashville, TN: Incentive Publications.

Carroll, C. (2010, Nov. 16). Why are new teachers leaving in droves? *The Guardian,* pp. 12, 16.

Clark, R. (2003). *The 55 essentials: An award-winning educator's rules for discovering the successful student in every child.* New York, NY: Hyperion.

Coloroso, B. (2002). *Kids are worth it!* (Rev. ed.). New York, NY: HarperCollins Publishers Inc.

Comer, J. (1995). *Poverty and learning: Nine powerful practices.* Lecture given at Education Service Center, Region 11, Houston, TX.

Crick, N., & Grotpeter, J. (1995). Relational aggression, gender, and social-psychology adjustment. *Child Development, 66(3),* 710–722.

Cullum, A. (2000). *The geranium on the windowsill just died but teacher you went right on.* Paris: Harlin Quist Books.

Curwin, R. L., & Mendler, A. N. (1988). *Discipline with dignity*. Alexandria, VA: Association for Supervision and Curriculum Development. (Note: The 3rd edition was published in 2008.)

Davis, J. (2006). Research at the margins: Dropping out of high school and mobility among African American males. *International Journal of Qualitative Studies in Education, 19*, 289–304.

Decker, D. M., Dona, D. P., & Christenson, S. L. (2007). Behaviorally at-risk African-American students: The importance of student–teacher relationships for student outcomes. *Journal of School Psychology, 45(1)*, 83–109.

Delpit, L. (1995). *Other people's children: Cultural conflict in the classroom*. New York, NY: New Press.

Dreikurs, R. (2004). *Discipline without tears: How to reduce conflict and establish cooperation in the classroom*. Mississauga, ON: Wiley.

Elliott, C. (1971). Noise tolerance and extraversion in children. *British Journal of Psychology, 62(3)*, 375–380.

Erlauer, L. (2003). *The brain-compatible classroom*. Alexandria, VA: Association for Supervision and Curriculum Development.

Esquith, R. (2007). *Teach like your hair's on fire*. New York, NY: Viking.

Frye, D. (2010). Engaging parents beyond back-to-school night. *National Writing Project*. Retrieved from www.nwp.org/cs/public/print/resource/2962

Furrer, C., & Skinner, E. A. (2003). Sense of relatedness as a factor in children's academic engagement and performance. *Journal of Educational Psychology, 95(1)*, 148–162.

Garfield, S. L. (1994). Research on client variables in psychotherapy. In A. E. Bergin & S. Garfield (Eds.), *Handbook of psychotherapy and behavior change* (4th ed., pp. 190-228). New York: Wiley.

Gerlach, J. M. (1994). Is this collaboration? In K. Bosworth & S. J. Hamilton (Eds.), *New Directions for Teaching and Learning, No. 59. Collaborative learning: Underlying processes and effective techniques* (pp. 5-14). San Francisco, CA: Jossey-Bass, 1994.

Ginott, H. (1972). *Teacher and child*. New York, NY: Avon Books.

Goldfried, M. R., Greenberg, L. S., & Marmar, C. (1990). Individual psychotherapy: Process and outcome. *Annual Review of Psychology, 41*, 659–688.

Goodenow, C. (1993). Classroom belonging among early adolescent students: Relationships to motivation and achievement. *Journal of Early Adolescence, 13(1)*, 21–43.

Grayson, J., & Alvarez, H. (2008). School climate factors relating to teacher burnout: A mediator model. *Teaching and Teacher Education, 24(5)*, 1349–1363.

Haberman, M. (1995). *STAR teachers of children in poverty*. Bloomington, IN: Kappa Delta Pi.

Hall, P. S., & Hall, N. D. (2003). Building relationships with challenging children. *Educational Leadership, 61(1)*, 60–63.

Hanna, F. J., Hanna, C. A., & Keys, S. G. (1999). Fifty strategies for counseling defiant and aggressive adolescents: Reaching, accepting, and relating. *Journal of Counseling and Development, 77(4)*, 395–404.

Hines, M. T. (2010). *Black kids & classroom management*. Temecula, CA: The Alexis Austin Group.

Hurren, B. L. (2010). *Humor in school is serious business*. Nashville, TN: Incentive Publications.

Hymel, S., et al. (2006). Reading, 'riting, 'rithmetic and relationships: Considering the social side of education. *Exceptionality Education Canada, 16(3)*, pp. 149–192.

Ingersoll, R. (2001). Teacher turnover and teacher shortages: An organizational analysis. *American Educational Research Journal, 38*(3), 499–534.

Inglish, P. (2012). *Top 10 reasons employees get fired.* Retrieved from http://hubpages.com/hub/Fired

Jackson, R. (2009). *Never work harder than your students & other principles of great teaching.* Alexandria, VA: Association for Supervision and Curriculum Development.

Jensen, E. (2010). *Top 10 brain-based teaching strategies.* Alexandria, VA: Association for Supervision and Curriculum Development.

Johnson, D. W., Johnson, R. T., & Houlubec, E. J. (1994). *New circles of learning: Cooperation in the classroom and school.* Alexandria, VA: Association for Supervision and Curriculum Development.

Juvonen, J., Nishina, A., & Graham, S. (2002). Peer harassment, psychological adjustment, and school functioning in early adolescence. *Journal of Educational Psychology, 92*(2), 349–359.

Kagan, S. (1994). *Cooperative learning.* San Clemente, CA: Kagan Publishing.

Kaiser Family Foundation (2006). *Zero to six: Electronic media in the lives of infants, toddlers, and preschoolers.* Retrieved from www.kff.org/entmedia/3378.cfm

Kleinfeld, J. (1975). Effective teachers of Eskimo and Indian students. *School Review, 83*(2), 301–344.

Konishi, C., Hymel, S., Zumbo, B. D., & Li, Zhen (2007). Do school bullying and student–teacher relations matter for academic achievement? *Canadian Journal of School Psychology, 25*(1), 19–39.

Kounin, J. (1977). *Discipline and group management in classrooms.* New York, NY: Holt, Rinehart, and Winston.

Kunjufu, J. (2002). *Black students, middle class teachers.* Chicago, IL: African American images.

Ladson-Billings, G. (2009). *The dreamkeepers: Successful teachers of African American children* (2nd ed.). San Francisco, CA: Jossey-Bass.

Lemov, D. (2010). *Teach like a champion: 49 techniques that put students on the path to college.* San Francisco, CA: Jossey-Bass.

Luiselli, J., et al. (2005). Whole-school positive behavior support: Effects on student discipline problems and academic performance. *Educational Psychology, 25*(2-3), 183–198.

Marzano, R. J., & Marzano, J. S. (2003). The key to classroom management. *Educational Leadership, 61*(1), 6–13.

McBride, B. (2009). *If they can argue well, they can write well.* Nashville, TN: Incentive Publications. (Note: A revised edition was published by World Book Inc./Incentive Publications in 2014.)

McCombs, B. L. (2004). The learner-centered psychological principles: A framework for balancing academic achievement and social-emotional learning outcomes. In J. Zins, R. Weissberg, M. Wang, and H. Walberg (Eds.), *Building academic success on social and emotional learning: What does the research say?* (pp. 23–39). New York, NY: Teachers College Press.

Mordock, J. B. (1991). *Counseling the defiant child.* New York, NY: Crossroad Publishing.

If You Can't Manage Them . . .

Orlinsky, D., Grawe, K., & Parks, B. (1994). Process and outcome in psychotherapy. In A. E. Bergin & S. L. Garfield (Eds.), *Handbook of psychotherapy and behavior change* (4th ed., pp. 270–376). New York: Wiley.

Patrick, H., Hicks, L., & Ryan, A. M. (1997). Relations of perceived social efficacy and social goal pursuit to self-efficacy for academic work. *Journal of Early Adolescence, 17*(2), 109–128.

Payne, R. (1996). *A framework for understanding poverty.* Highlands, TX: Aha! Process, Inc. (Note: The 4th edition was published in 2005.)

Prensky, M. (2010). *Teaching digital natives: Partnering for real learning.* Thousand Oaks, CA: Corwin Press.

Rideout, V. J., Foehr, U., & Roberts, D. (2010). *Generation M2: Media in the lives of 8- to 18-year-olds.* Menlo Park, CA: Henry J. Kaiser Family Foundation.

Rogers, S., & Renard, L. (1999). Relationship-driven teaching. *Educational Leadership, 57*(1), 34–37.

Rosenblum-Lowden, R. (1997). *You have to go to school . . . you're the teacher!* Thousand Oaks, CA: Corwin Press, Inc. (Note: The 3rd edition was published in 2008.)

Sax, L. (2005). *Why gender matters: What parents and teachers need to know about the emerging science of sex differences.* New York, NY: Random House Inc.

Schaps, E., et al. (2004). Community in school as key to student growth: Findings from the Child Development Project. In J. Zins, R. Weissberg, M. Wang, & H. Walberg (Eds.), *Building academic success on social and emotional learning: What does the research say?* (pp. 189–205). New York, NY: Teachers College Press.

Sexton, T. L., & Whiston, S. C. (1994). The status of the counseling relationship: An empirical review, theoretical implications, and research directions. *The Counseling Psychologist, 22*(1), 6–78.

Slavin, R. (1995). *Cooperative learning: Theory, research, and practice* (2nd ed.). Boston, MA: Allyn & Bacon.

Spencer, J. (2008). *Everyone's invited! Interactive strategies that engage young adolescents.* Columbus, OH: National Middle School Association.

Walsh, D. (2004). *Why do they act that way? A survival guide to the adolescent brain for you and your teen.* New York, NY: Free Press.

Walsh, D. (2007). *No: Why kids—of all ages—need to hear it and ways parents can say it.* New York, NY: Free Press.

Wentzel, K. (1997). Student motivation in middle school: The role of perceived pedagogical caring. *Journal of Educational Psychology, 89*(3), 411–419.

Wentzel, K. (1998). Social relationships and motivation in middle school: The role of parents, teachers, and peers. *Journal of Educational Psychology, 90*(2), 202–209.

Wolk, S. (2003). Hearts and minds. *Educational Leadership, 61*(1), 14–18.

Wormeli, R. (2006). *Fair isn't always equal: Assessing & grading in the differentiated classroom.* Portland, ME: Stenhouse.

Zins, J., et al. (2004). The scientific base linking social and emotional learning to school success. In J. Zins, R. Weissberg, M. Wang, & H. Walberg (Eds.), *Building academic success on social and emotional learning: What does the research say?* (pp. 3–22). New York, NY: Teachers College Press.